The Big Mac Index

The Big Mac Index

Applications of Purchasing Power Parity

Li Lian Ong

First published 2003 by
PALGRAVE MACMILLAN
Houndmills, Basingstoke, Hampshire RG21 6XS and
175 Fifth Avenue, New York, N.Y. 10010
Companies and representatives throughout the world

PALGRAVE MACMILLAN is the global academic imprint of the Palgrave
Macmillan division of St. Martin's Press, LLC and of Palgrave Macmillan Ltd.
Macmillan® is a registered trademark in the United States, United Kingdom
and other countries. Palgrave is a registered trademark in the European
Union and other countries.

ISBN 1–4039–0310–7

This book is printed on paper suitable for recycling and made from fully
managed and sustained forest sources.

A catalogue record for this book is available from the British Library.

Library of Congress Cataloging-in-Publication Data

Ong, Li Lian.
    The Big Mac index : applications of purchasing power parity /
Li Lian Ong.
        p. cm.
    Includes bibliographical references and index.
    ISBN 1–4039–0310–7 (cloth)
    1. Purchasing power parity. 2. Foreign exchange rates. I. Title.
HG3821 .525 2002
332.4′1–dc21   2002033302

10   9   8   7   6   5   4   3   2
12 11 10 09 08 07 06 05 04

Printed and bound in Great Britain by
Antony Rowe Ltd, Chippenham and Eastbourne

For Mum and Dad

Contents

List of Tables

List of Figures

Foreword

In this book Li Lian Ong draws on her earlier doctoral research and more recent experience working in international financial markets to review and enhance the use of purchasing power parity (PPP), or relative prices, in the analysis of exchange rates.

PPP has a long history in academic and applied research. Despite obvious difficulties in utilizing it to forecast exchange rates in the very short term, reflecting the presence of a number of other influences including the increased role and volatility of market expectations, in particular concerning relative asset prices and changes in the stance of monetary policy, PPP continues to be used in economic analysis such as in the estimation of relative standards of living between countries.

For her analysis Li Lian adopts the popular *Big Mac* (hamburger) index, which was pioneered and is regularly updated by *The Economist* magazine, to outline a novel and potentially useful enhancement to PPP for use in understanding the likely trends in exchange rates.

The first two chapters of the book provide a comprehensive review of both the theory and past empirical research into PPP, and discuss the problems associated with estimating PPP exchange rates due to well-known complications associated with the measurement of relevant price series, market imperfections and structural change. The application of PPP to the determination of equilibrium exchange rates is also discussed, including the important question of the direction of causality between relative prices and exchange rates.

However, Li Lian's main focus is on the importance of *productivity bias* – or the differences across countries in rates of growth in productivity between the traded and non-traded sectors – when using PPP to estimate equilibrium exchange rates.

Her analysis in Chapter 3 first shows that the *Big Mac* index has been a generally reliable guide to the year-on-year trends in exchange rates, and even more so over the longer term. Nevertheless, several persistent discrepancies are identified, which she estimates are most importantly related to productivity differentials between countries. Li Lian adjusts for this bias by excluding the costs of those inputs that are not traded (basically services), which she estimates account on average for 93 per cent of the price of the hamburgers. Li Lian shows that this adjustment, and her resulting *No-Frills Index*, considerably enhances the tracking of exchange rates over the long term. While the use of hamburger prices to test the applicability of PPP to exchange rates may be challenged in terms of some of the measurement and conceptual issues reviewed in earlier chapters, this approach rather effectively combines a well-established and popular measure of the over- and undervaluation of currencies with differences in productivity growth, which has been a significant issue in recent economic debate about relative growth rates and standards of living. As such, it should appeal not only to economic researchers and policy-makers but also to those who must deal with exchange rate issues in day-to-day business decisions.

The final three chapters of Li Lian's book provide examples of how this approach can be used. Chapter 4 provides a brief assessment of the 1997 ASEAN currency crisis – extending Li Lian's analysis to include other countries affected by that and similar currency crises, for example Korea and Brazil, would broaden its appeal to policy-makers.

Two more business-oriented applications are discussed in Chapters 5 and 6, and may have more immediate appeal to potential users. In particular, the suggested application of this approach to the estimation of real costs of living and relocation expenses is relevant to the globalized nature of many business operations, and the inevitable consequences for costs as a consequence of increased staff mobility.

Li Lian's book makes a very useful addition to the literature on purchasing power parity by providing an enhanced approach for those who continue to apply PPP to the analysis of exchange rates, both what determines them and their consequences for economic policy and business decisions.

Bill Shields
Visiting Professor
Macquarie Graduate School of Management
Macquarie University, Sydney, Australia

Preface

In the course of purchasing power parity (PPP) research over the years, the debate has alternately boiled and simmered over the choice of appropriate ingredients for inclusion in the traditional 'basket of goods and services'. Amongst the items on the menu is a veritable smorgasbord of indices to whet the appetite of the PPP gourmet. The selection includes wholesale prices, consumer prices and gross domestic product price measures.

Not surprisingly, as I discuss in Chapter 1, researchers have made a meal of the argument over their accuracy for PPP purposes, given the different constituents in the mixture of goods and services that make up these indices. The extent to which these items spice up the application of PPP in exchange rate determination is covered in the discussion on index-number problems and the productivity bias hypothesis. Chapter 2 contemplates the 'explosion' in PPP research since the advent of floating exchange rates in the early 1970s, notwithstanding the controversy surrounding the topic. In particular, my co-author and I review the trends in research methods used in empirical tests of PPP during the 1990s, and the balance of findings in favour of PPP. We also discuss the rave reviews accorded *The Economist*'s Big Mac Index, as a quick and easy 'fast food' equivalent for measuring PPP, and the role it has played in stirring market interest in this area of research.

In Chapter 3, I demonstrate empirically that the Big Mac Index is a more palatable solution to the index-number problem, given that this hamburger is produced locally in more than 100 countries around the world, with only minor changes in recipe, and thus has the flavour of 'the perfect universal commodity'. The productivity bias problem inherent in this area of research – wherein the existence of non-traded goods in the 'basket' results in inaccurate measures of PPP – is also addressed by slicing out the non-traded portion of the Big Mac. Chapter 4 is a vignette on how 'burgernomics' could have been applied to predict accurately the Asian currency crisis in 1997 – and the Mexican peso standoff in 1995 – where more traditional economic measures failed. The results confirm that these currencies did indeed get their just desserts when their peg to the US$ was removed.

The icing on the cake is that the Big Mac Index also has more practical, day-to-day applications, as discussed in Chapter 5. The Index, rather than the more volatile exchange rates, should be used for more accurate comparison between salaries and costs-of-living in different countries around the world, as it better represents the purchasing power equivalents in each country. This is especially useful for economic migrants and expatriates working for multinational corporations. In Chapter 6, my co-author and I use the academic profession as an example of how a relocating professor should weigh up remuneration incentives, as well as intrinsic factors such as the quality of life.

LI LIAN ONG

Acknowledgements

The material in this book was written while my contributors and I were at the University of Western Australia. The views expressed in this book do not reflect those of my current employer, the International Monetary Fund. All mistakes remain my responsibility.

I would very much like to thank:

Professor H. Y. Izan and Professor Kenneth W. Clements at the University of Western Australia for all their help, encouragement and support.

Yihui Lan and Jason D. Mitchell for their indispensable collaboration.

The Department of Accounting and Finance and the Economic Research Centre at the University of Western Australia, for providing research infrastructure and funding.

The Australian Agency for International Development for providing postgraduate research scholarship.

Paul Lloyd for invaluable computing support, and Margaret Ledgerton and Kael Driscoll for data assistance.

Caitlin Cornish, my commissioning editor at Palgrave Macmillan, for her patience and advice throughout the publication process.

Colleagues in academia for providing useful comments on the material in this book.

Notes on the Contributors

Yihui Lan completed her PhD in economics at the University of Western Australia. Her thesis, 'The Long-Term Behaviour of Exchange Rates', uses Big Mac data to test the theory of purchasing power parity and to derive the long-run values of currencies. Yihui had previously obtained her undergraduate degree from the Huazhong University of Science and Technology, in China.

Jason D. Mitchell is Assistant Professor of Finance at the Hong Kong Polytechnic University. He has previously held appointments at the University of Western Australia and the University of Sydney, and has also worked as an accountant in Perth, Western Australia. Jason obtained his Bachelor of Commerce, Master of Accounting and Doctor of Philosophy in international finance at the University of Western Australia, and is a Chartered Accountant with the Institute of Chartered Accountants in Australia. He has published research in behavioural finance, capital structure and corporate reconstruction, valuation methods and issues, exchange rates and energy pricing.

1
Purchasing Power Parity: A Survey of the Issues

The purchasing power parity (PPP) doctrine, one of the most widely researched areas in international finance, is also probably one of the most controversial in the theory of exchange rate determination. According to the theory of purchasing power parity, the rate of exchange between two currencies is determined by the differences in the price levels of their respective countries. However, while proponents of the theory argue that PPP provides a strong basis for determining exchange rates, others have contended otherwise, with a plethora of empirical research demonstrating persistent deviations from PPP. Consequently, we provide a survey of the issues that contribute to the problems in testing the theory. Notably, factors such as the lack of uniformity in the price indices used to determine the long-run equilibrium exchange rate – also known as the 'index-number problem' – and the issue of productivity bias, which is probably seen as the most serious criticism of PPP theory, are discussed. We also consider the role of market imperfections as well as structural changes in the economy.

Introduction

The origins of PPP theory can be traced back to Spanish scholars of the sixteenth century, although the intellectual origins of the doctrine are credited to Wheatley's and Ricardo's work in the nineteenth century.[1] The PPP theory as we know it today, however, is attributed to Gustav Cassel's writings during the 1920s. Cassel was instrumental in rekindling interest in PPP theory during the modern era, after its demise in the latter part of the nineteenth century.[2] This interest has intensified over the last two decades with the collapse of the Bretton Woods system and the reintroduction of flexible exchange rates in the early 1970s.[3]

The relationship between exchange rates and prices that is summarized by the PPP doctrine is considered one of the oldest, and possibly the most controversial, in the theory of exchange rate determination. Frenkel (1981) attributes much of the controversy to the fact that the PPP theory does not specify the precise mechanism by which exchange rates are related to prices, nor the precise conditions that must be satisfied in order for the doctrine to be correct. In short, he claims that it merely shows a relationship between two variables without explaining how such a relationship comes about. Other researchers have also suggested that the choice of price indices used in empirical tests, and market imperfections such as transportation and transaction costs, contribute to the problems surrounding the theory. On the other hand, some authors contend that PPP does provide a strong basis for exchange rate determination, with useful policy implications.

As a precursor to our own research in this area, we will first review the issues relating to our research design. The next section looks at the definitions and concepts of PPP itself, after which we deal with the index-number problem and the concept of exchange rate equilibrium, respectively. We then discuss the *productivity bias hypothesis*, which is generally accepted as the most important reason for departures from PPP, and other limitations of PPP. This is followed by a summary.

Absolute and relative parities

PPP required that the price level in two countries be equal when converted to a common currency to ensure that the *real* exchange rate is equal to unity. Consequently, any change in the *nominal* exchange rate would be determined by a change in the price level. Thus, it could be said that the PPP theory of exchange rates looks at the *relationship* between a country's foreign exchange rate and its price level, as well as the relationship between the *changes* in those variables.

PPP may be expressed in either absolute or relative terms. *Absolute PPP* is the ratio of price levels which are measured as the number of units of currency per unit of physical quantity. Since absolute PPP of the foreign currency is the ratio of the domestic price level to the foreign price level, it has as its dimension the number of units of domestic currency per unit of foreign currency. In turn, *relative PPP* is based on price *movements* which are measured by price indices relative to a designated base period. The basic concept here is that the change in the exchange rate should equal the inflation differential. It can either be defined as the ratio of the domestic to the foreign price index, or the product of this ratio and the base-period exchange rate. Relative PPP implies that the real exchange rate is constant, although it need not be unity. This means that movements in the real exchange rate are synonymous with deviations from PPP.

Officer (1982) defines the absolute and relative versions of PPP as follows: absolute PPP is represented by P_{ct}/P_t^*, where P_{ct} and P_t^* are the domestic and foreign price levels, respectively, in period t; relative PPP (first concept) is represented by I_{ct}/I_{ct}^*, where I_{ct} and I_{ct}^* are the domestic and foreign price indices, calculated as $(P_{ct}/P_{c,t-1})$ and $\left(P_t^*/P_{c,t-1}^*\right)$, respectively; and relative PPP (second concept) is represented by $I_{ct}/I_{ct}^* \cdot R_0$, where R_0 is the number of units of domestic currency per unit of foreign currency for the base period. This definition of PPP is only equal to the absolute form of PPP, presumed to be the new equilibrium exchange rate, if the changes in the economies that occurred since the base period are purely monetary in nature (Cassel, 1922). In other words, it is only in the case of a uniform inflation where all prices are unaltered in their relation to one another that the relative PPP (second concept) necessarily equals the absolute PPP for that period.

Cassel (1928) observes that the construction of absolute PPP would only allow a precise comparison of price levels in two countries if, and only if, all corresponding prices differ by the same multiplicative factor. In practice, differing relative prices yield only 'an approximate comparison' (p. 8) between the purchasing power of both currencies. Thus, the use of appropriate indices, wherein individual commodities are weighted according to their economic importance, is advocated. The weighting pattern should reflect either the production or consumption of these commodities.

The index-number problem

Frankel (1994, p. 4) states that, 'If purchasing power parity held among currencies, the proper test would be a simple matter of identifying the price index of the appropriate international basket of goods consumed by investors, and measuring asset returns in terms of it.' However, in the course of PPP research there has been much argument over what constitutes an *appropriate* price index for making PPP comparisons. Amongst the possibilities that have been mooted are the wholesale price index (WPI), cost-of-living (COL) price measures, the consumer price index (CPI) and gross domestic product (GDP).

Cassel (1921, p. 110), for instance, suggests that the WPI would be 'a fairly reliable index of the movements of the general level of prices' when 'prices have adjusted themselves to one another so as to make the prices of products correspond to their cost of production'. Consequently, the level of wages in an economy could be a very important factor in determining the value of its currency in the long run (Cassel, 1922). However, Keynes (1930) opposes the use of the WPI to calculate PPP as it is heavily weighted with traded goods. He contends that this would result in a truism since the computed relative price parities would then be almost equal to the actual exchange rate, thus providing spurious verification of the theory. This is consistent with Cassel (1922) who had previously opposed the use of price indices relating solely to traded goods for several reasons: (1) they are 'limited to a small class of commodities, and are therefore subject to variations' (p. 47); (2) ambiguity exists in the definition of traded and non-traded goods (hereafter T and N respectively), given that small changes in the exchange rate may result in one becoming the other; and (3) the applicability of the law of one price to traded goods implies that they tend to move together regardless of the deviation from PPP.

In determining the relationship between PPPs, exchange rates and income levels, Balassa (1964) also acknowledges the index-number problem. He, too, argues against the use of WPIs in determining a cause-and-effect relationship between exchange rates and PPPs, since the heavy weighting given to T would mean that as T moves towards a world price, the prices reflect changes in world markets rather than domestic inflationary pressures. This follows Yeager (1958) who had previously suggested that causation is stronger from price levels to exchange rates than vice versa, since trade flows are known to have only minor effects on domestic prices. Furthermore, since movements in the general price level are generally determined by changes in the money supply rather than exchange rate movements, use of the WPI would not accurately reflect PPP.

Balassa subsequently finds that his results are dependent on the choice of weights used, in this case the final bill of goods consumed in individual countries. For example, by using one country's consumption pattern as weights, as against another's, the purchasing power of the latter's currency would be underestimated; the latter's currency would be overestimated if its own consumption weights are used. As a solution, Balassa proposes using the geometric average of the two weights, although he concedes that 'this average lacks a specific economic meaning' (p. 587).

If the law of one price holds for every individual good, then it follows that it must hold for any *identical* basket of goods. Froot and Rogoff (1995), however, find that most empirical tests do not attempt to compare identical baskets, but instead use different countries' CPIs and WPIs, which consist of different weights and mixes of goods across countries. Thus, they observe that even if PPP holds, it may not necessarily show up in the results if these indices are used, unless the two countries in question have identical baskets. They suggest the use of *price differentials*, where changes in relative price levels are offset by changes in the exchange rate. Similarly, Betton *et al.* (1995) observe that when consumption bundles are not identical, price indices based on local consumption patterns may behave differently even though the law of one price holds for each commodity. They suggest that measures of inflation differentials and price level ratios are intrinsically subject to error when price indices are based on different baskets of goods, resulting in biased outcomes of PPP tests. This is supported by Kravis *et al.* (1975), who previously recalculated foreign inflation using US weights in the foreign price indices. Their results demonstrate far stronger support for PPP than those using traditionally constructed indices.

Other research based on the use of CPIs includes Frenkel and Mussa (1980), who observe that short-run changes in exchange rates bear little relationship to short-run differentials in national inflation rates, particularly those measured by CPIs. Adler and Dumas (1983) discover that inflation differentials in the 1970s explain less than 5 per cent of monthly exchange rate movements, which means that 95 per cent of currency movements are *not* caused by current inflation. Meanwhile, Frenkel (1981) and Kravis and Lipsey (1978) find that there has been no close correlation between movements in exchange rates and movements in the ratio of national price levels, especially in the 1970s when it had been close to zero.

In his paper, Miller (1984, p. 354) observes that the use of different price indices for parity calculation purposes 'might conceivably yield different conclusions concerning the validity of PPP ... [s]ince the consumer price index, the wholesale price index and the GDP deflator all use different weighting patterns ...'. Furthermore, he argues that since the prices of individual commodities have increased at different rates, the various indices often reflect substantially different rates of inflation. He concludes that it is 'therefore possible that one's choice of price index has a considerable bearing on the conclusions'. It is suspected that this problem would have been exacerbated during the 1970s when world economies experienced large changes in relative prices.

Williamson (1983, pp. 19–20) supports the idea of 'a measure that is able to diverge ... only as the competitive position of the tradable sector changes', as opposed to consumer prices rising relative to the price of T as a result of rapid productivity growth in the latter. This criterion, he declares, rules out the use of export and consumer prices, and instead lends support to the use of *wholesale prices of manufacturing output*. He eventually settles for a combined index incorporating the geometric means of WPIs and unit labour costs, which is consistent with Cassel's (1922) position on the importance of wage levels discussed earlier.

Sjaastad (1991, pp. 1–2) contends that PPP research is often 'plagued by difficulties in measuring the key underlying variables' in that inaccurate use of broadly defined price levels and the existence of exchange rate controls have complicated the interpretation of any subsequent results. In this particular study, he separates the 'pure' from the 'measurement' error by isolating and quantifying the measurement error component. He considers the Swiss case ideal for this purpose as it has basically had a freely floating exchange rate and a stable commercial policy throughout the post-Bretton Woods period.

Sjaastad's interpretation of PPP allows for changes in relative prices that are not a consequence of the exchange rate. He relates PPP with the behaviour of the exchange rate relative to N prices and foreign-currency prices of T, rather than with domestic and foreign price levels. Using both the bilateral real exchange rate (which is based on two currencies and two respective price levels) and the multilateral real exchange rate (which reflects internal relative prices) in his tests, he finds that the measurement errors are mainly attributed to the use of the bilateral real exchange rate for several reasons. Firstly, the US price level measures a broader set of goods and services than the Swiss index. This means that the price of Swiss T can rise or fall relative to the US price level simply because different weights are given to different commodity groups within the respective indices, which will induce deviations from PPP when relative prices change.[4] Secondly, the degree of influence exerted by the US price level and the dollar exchange rate over the US dollar price of Swiss T also plays an important role in determining measurement errors. This influence is dependent on the degree to which the US dominates the market for Swiss T. Overall, Sjaastad finds strong support for PPP by showing that the high volatility of the US dollar–Swiss franc exchange rate since 1973 has failed to destabilize the Swiss price level; rather, it is due to corresponding variability in the dollar prices of Swiss T. He strongly concludes that 'in the Swiss case, at least, the bulk of the variance in the bilateral real exchange rate is measurement error, pure and simple' (p. 39).

Other supporters of a broader price measure include the asset-market proponents, who theorize that the exchange rate equilibrates by equalizing the PPP of domestic and foreign currencies, *via* arbitrage involving the currencies of these two economies. One suggestion is the use of COL price measures. The advantages of this measure are that (1) costs of production are less subject to exchange rate changes than are prices of T; (2) costs are more likely to be representative of long-run prices (for absolute parity) and reflective of permanent changes in prices (for relative parity) than are product prices, since they exclude the volatile profit component; and (3) the sale of T at world prices which incurs losses (profits) could explain currency overvaluation (undervaluation). Artus (1978) suggests that the cost–parity concept is more appropriate since the structure of factor prices (in the form of wages) within a country changes less over time than the structure of commodity prices. This makes the relative prices of N, as represented by the former, more stable than those of the latter. He also finds that wage rates in the T sector are less vulnerable to direct foreign influences than are commodity prices in the same sector.

Frenkel (1981), on the other hand, argues that the choice of price indices is immaterial as long as the *structure of relative prices* in the economy remains stable, as when the shocks are of a monetary origin. It only becomes of critical importance when there are *real* shocks which alter relative prices. These shocks result in the presence of secular trends due to shifts in rates of technological change, commercial policies, product mix and commodity-price shocks. Frenkel observes that changes in internal relative prices would be picked up by changes in the ratio of the COL index to the WPI, since the COL index contains relatively more N than the WPI. His tests show that the internal price structure was relatively stable for the US and UK, somewhat changed for Germany, and highly volatile for France during the 1970s. He subsequently attributes the collapse of PPP during that time to this instability in internal relative prices.

Previous to that, Frenkel (1978) had used alternative price indices, namely wholesale, material and food, to test the absolute and relative versions of PPP during the floating rate period of the 1920s. Overall, he finds that both versions of PPP hold for that period, save a couple of exceptions. Upon the incorporation of lags into his model, he finds the estimated long-run elasticities of the exchange rate with respect to the price ratio to be about unity; the short-run elasticities, however, vary across exchange rates and price indices. Furthermore, the speed of adjustment for the material price indices appears to exceed that of the WPIs.

The preceding debate notwithstanding, ultimately, as Cassel (1922) suggests, a *general* price level is required to define absolute PPP, while a *general* price index should be used for relative PPP. This is because only general index figures would encompass, as far as possible, the entire range of commodities available in an economy. In today's terms, this would mean using the gross domestic product (GDP) price level and the GDP deflator to derive the relative and absolute versions of PPP, respectively. Cassel (1932) further justifies the use of a relative PPP approach, as opposed to absolute PPP, since he considers measures of price levels to be practically impossible to obtain for the latter.

Like Cassel, Officer (1974) also advocates the use of the GDP measure, although for a different reason. He argues that GDP is appropriate since it represents each country's pattern of production, which is ideal for weighting purposes in constructing a price measure. Furthermore, since PPP theory is concerned with prices and production within the boundaries of respective countries, GDP is preferred to gross national product (GNP) as it comprises domestic rather than national production. In practice, however, PPP computations using GNP differ minimally from GDP (Officer, 1982).

Determining the equilibrium exchange rate

According to Cassel (1926), absolute PPP is the main determinant of the equilibrium exchange rate (EER); that is, the rate that results in a current account equilibrium. He argues that if the actual exchange rate, defined as the price of foreign currency in terms of domestic currency, exceeds (falls below) the equilibrium rate, then the domestic country would have a trade surplus (deficit). A trade balance is achieved when the actual rate is at equilibrium.

Frankel (1985) proposes six possible reasons as to why disequilibrium in the exchange rate may occur. However, based on available evidence he is able to rule out five of the six possible explanations and posits that 'overshooting' is the most plausible explanation for observed exchange rate behaviour. Although associated with exchange rate volatility, it is consistent with market efficiency in that one cannot expect to make arbitrage profits from this phenomenon. The dynamics of overshooting come from variables that are 'sticky'; that is, variables that do not react instantaneously to changes in the economy even though these changes are reflected in the exchange rate initially. Gradual adjustments of these variables (for example, prices, level of domestic claims on foreign assets and current account balances) eventually result in the reversal of the initial change in the exchange rate.

Dornbusch's (1976) findings on the effects of monetary (or nominal) shocks and sticky prices on exchange rates are supported by the high correlation between real and nominal exchange rate changes, during both fixed and flexible exchange rate regimes. The fact that observed fluctuations in the real exchange rate are greater under flexible rates is due to the higher volatility of nominal exchange rates under this regime, while price levels remain sluggish under either regime. However, as Stockman (1987, 1988) notes, these are not the only plausible explanations for observed movements in the real and nominal rates. Shocks to technology, tastes, and trade and fiscal policies are also responsible for real exchange rate movements under both fixed and flexible regimes. These shocks are also reflected in the nominal exchange rates instead of relative price levels because of the price stabilization policies pursued by monetary authorities.

Using 130 years of data for the US and UK, Rogers (1995) finds evidence to support both the 'sticky-prices view' of real exchange rate determination, which emphasizes nominal shocks, and the 'equilibrium view', which emphasizes real shocks in the economy. He suggests that real and monetary shocks account for approximately the same percentage of the variance in the real exchange rate in the short term, although the effects of the latter do not persist over the long run. He is also able to separate the sources of the shocks into demand shock (real) and equal amounts of money multiplier shocks and monetary base shocks (monetary).

Officer (1982, p. 15) defines the long-run EER as 'the fixed exchange rate that yields balance of payments equilibrium over a certain time period'. He further suggests that the time period should incorporate both seasonal and cyclical fluctuations in the balance of payments, as well as business cycles at home and abroad. When PPP is used to measure disequilibrium in a floating exchange rate, the implication is that some force is keeping the exchange rate away from its long-run equilibrium, which should equal the PPP. The short-run EER, in turn, is merely that which would exist under a freely floating exchange rate system; that is, one that is completely unmanaged by any institution.

The above concepts are reflected in Officer's three propositions of PPP theory. The first states that PPP is the principal determinant of the long-run exchange rate, such that the long-run EER tends to equal PPP. Secondly, the long-run EER is seen to be the principal determinant of, and tends to be approached by, the short-run EER. Given that the short-run EER approaches the long-run EER, which in turn converges on the PPP, the third proposition follows that the short-run EER must also be determined by PPP. In a nutshell, this means that PPP *should* hold in the long run. Consistent with these propositions, Manzur (1990) finds that PPP performs poorly in the short run, but that the long-run evidence is consistent with the PPP hypothesis. In this instance, the transition from the short run to the long run appears to take five years.

Krugman (1990a) discusses EER in the context of the equilibrium *real* exchange rate. He sees adjustments to this real rate as being a function of time and nominal exchange rate policy. These equilibrium real exchange rate shifts are attributed to several sources. One possible factor is the existence of real shocks, and international capital flows are another, albeit more contentious, source of shifts in the equilibrium real exchange rate. Capital flows, which are predictably temporary, are said to result in a potential decline in the equilibrium real exchange rate. The argument here is that an economy which is the temporary recipient of capital inflows will see a rise in the demand for its N as well as its T, resulting in a general increase in prices on world markets and a corresponding fall in the real exchange rate to restore equilibrium. Krugman also finds evidence that nominal shocks do, in the short run, cause real exchange rate changes, and that their effects are quite persistent.

Williamson (1983, p. 5) views misalignment in the real exchange rate as 'a persistent departure from its long-run equilibrium level'. He contends that misalignment does not preclude the market from clearing; that is, demand for a particular currency equating its supply. Broadly speaking, there are three concepts of equilibrium: market equilibrium, current equilibrium and fundamental equilibrium. Market equilibrium exists when demand equals supply in the absence of official intervention, at the nominal level. Using this concept, non-intervention implies equilibrium. Like market equilibrium, the current equilibrium rate refers to a nominal rate whose adjustments occur in response to 'news'. Accordingly, this is 'the rate that would obtain if markets had full knowledge of all relevant facts and acted rationally to that knowledge' (Williamson, 1983, p. 16). It is dependent on factors such as interest rates, which in turn are dependent on macroeconomic policy, the state of the business cycle and net asset positions *vis-à-vis* other economies.

Fundamental equilibrium occurs when the exchange rate is that justified by fundamentals. This concept of equilibrium relates to the *real* exchange rate; that is, the inflation-adjusted exchange rate. According to Williamson (1983, p. 14), it is the exchange rate 'which is expected to generate a current account surplus or deficit equal to the underlying capital flow over the cycle, given that the country is pursuing "internal balance" as best it can and not restricting trade for balance of payments reasons'. This fundamental equilibrium exchange rate (hereafter FEER) is equivalent to that referred to previously by Krugman and Officer as the EER.[5] References to currency over-/undervaluation are usually made within the context of this particular form of equilibrium. These changes to the FEER occur as a result of changes to either the underlying capital flow, or the demand and supply of traded goods. In turn, changes in the latter are usually a result of productivity growth differentials, exploitation of significant new resources or permanent exogenous changes in the terms of trade. The issue of productivity differentials and its significance for PPP will be discussed in detail in the next section.

Consistent with Williamson's definition, Pick and Volrath (1994, p. 555) posit that real exchange rate misalignment occurs when 'actual exchange rates are not allowed to adjust to changes in economic fundamentals'. They perceive factors such as unsustainable monetary, fiscal and various trade and exchange control policies to be the principal causes of misalignment. In quantifying the effects of exchange rate misalignment on developing-country agricultural export performance, they use Edwards' (1989) real exchange rate model to show that such misalignment has a significantly adverse impact on those exports. The results provide support for the argument that exchange rate misalignment could adversely affect the economic growth and export performance of developing countries, thus emphasizing the importance of sustainable macroeconomic policies.

Bartolini (1995, p. 47) suggests that the 'difficulty of assessing the dynamics of equilibrium real exchange rates, combined with statistical problems such as constructing qualitatively homogeneous baskets of goods and services, is central to any analysis of competitiveness'. However, he argues that temporary deviations of exchange rates from their medium- or long-run equilibrium may not necessitate policy intervention, as they are not necessarily a result of market failure. Rather, they may actually be a reflection of optimal market responses to numerous exogeneous shocks.

The productivity bias hypothesis

The *productivity bias hypothesis* (PBH) is probably considered the most serious criticism of the absolute PPP theory today. This hypothesis is based on the premise that productivity growth in the T sector is faster than that in the N sector. Bartolini (1995, p. 47) observes that

> differential rates of technical change in the traded and non-traded sectors have long been recognised as a cause of sustained movements in equilibrium real exchange rates and, therefore, as a reason for the persistent failure of PPP. This is because, while market competition may keep prices of tradeables broadly aligned internationally, prices of non-tradeables need not move together in different countries.

Thus, assuming that the productivity of T increases while that of N remains constant, the existence of world prices for real interest rates and T means that the productivity increase is matched by a real wage increase that keeps the marginal cost of T constant, while increasing the marginal cost of N and hence their price. It is obvious then that the increase in the relative price of N reflects different productivity growth rates between the two sectors. The result is that if the real exchange rate between two countries is computed using price deflators that include both T and N, then the currency of the country with faster productivity growth in the T than in the N sector will be systematically overvalued relative to its PPP level.[6]

Balassa (1964, pp. 587–8) asserts that, 'international productivity differences in the service sector are considerably smaller than in the production of traded goods, raising thereby the cost of services in high-income countries'. His examination of seven major industrial countries confirms that productivity increases in the services sector are lower than those for the national economy as a whole. He regresses the ratio of PPP to the official exchange rate on per capita GNP for 12 industrial countries, to test the hypothesis that higher levels of service prices in rich countries result in systematic differences between PPPs and EERs. He finds a significant positive correlation between the two variables.

Although the PBH is generally credited to Balassa (1964) and Samuelson (1964), earlier work on the subject includes that of Hagen (1957), Harrod (1939) and Rothschild (1958). Cassel himself (1932) had earlier commented on the fact that services are relatively more expensive in richer countries. Harrod (1939) classifies the goods produced by a country as A, B, and C goods. He defines A goods as staple goods of homogeneous character and capable of entering into foreign trade. Transportation costs aside, these international goods trade at a common world price. At the other extreme, C goods and services are those that are, by nature, incapable of entering into international trade. There is no international price for C goods. Quasi-international B goods fall in the intermediate position between the two, and although there is a tendency towards a common world price, complete uniformity is rarely achieved.

It is Harrod's contention that when C goods are incorporated into the calculations, the theory of PPP would only hold true in the extreme circumstance where, among other things, the ratio of efficiency in producing C goods to A goods is the same in two countries and the rewards to factors of production – or their ratio in A industries to those in C industries – are the same in both countries. In practice, these conditions would be highly unlikely, given the different levels of technological progress in each country and the expertise of human resources available. According to Harrod, 'the movement of scientific knowledge, business ability and industrial skill is extremely slow and sticky' (p. 73).

Rothschild (1958) is the first author to empirically test the PBH. He states that the purchasing power equivalents (implied exchange rates) would normally yield exchange rates which are less favourable than the equilibrium to the richer country. Furthermore, the greater the productivity differential between the rich and poor countries, the greater the differential between the price of N, and thus the larger the deviation from the EER. Using, alternately, the US and Germany as standard countries for tests of cross-sectional data, his results show that the ratio of absolute PPP to actual exchange rate is positively related to per capita GNP, and that the deviation between PPP and the exchange rate is much higher for T than for N. Both these findings are consistent with the PBH.

However, subsequent studies by Clague and Tanzi (1972) and de Vries (1968), among others, have failed to reproduce statistically significant results similar to Balassa's (1964). Officer (1974, p. 874) questions the validity of the PBH because it ignores 'the difference in the qualities of the services' among countries. Improving on Balassa's apparent methodological weaknesses, Officer (1976b) subsequently provides statistical evidence that the PBH lacks firm empirical foundation. He does, however, concede that 'the most important reason for a systematic divergence between PPP and the equilibrium rate is the existence of productivity differences between countries' (p. 545).

Clements and Semudram (1983) use three different sets of data to test Balassa's (1964) hypothesis: the price of haircuts, which Samuelson (1964) describes as a classic non-traded good; multi-commodity prices for 15 countries; and relative price movements of N in nine countries. Their results demonstrate a clear positive correlation between the price of a haircut and GDP, which supports the argument that N are relatively more expensive in richer countries. Analysis of Voltaire and Stack's (1980) results, which are based on data from Kravis *et al.* (1978), show that food (which is a traded good) becomes cheaper relative to recreation (a non-traded good) as they move from poorer to richer countries. Using Goldstein and Officer's (1979) time-series data, the authors find the income elasticity of the ratio of N prices to T prices to be significantly positive, thus corroborating the cross-sectional results that N become relatively more expensive with increasing per capita income.

Recently, one method of accounting for departures from PPP has received wide attention. As with Balassa and many others after him, this method produced by the United Nations International Comparisons Project (ICP) is also based on the premise of productivity differentials between countries, as well as 'factor proportion' differentials.[7] According to Kravis (1986), new insights into the world economy have arisen with the use of PPPs to replace exchange rates in converting GDP and its components to a common currency. He claims that this system of international income and purchasing power comparisons improves the measurement of countries' average incomes and the differences between them. He argues that the exchange rate is not a reliable indicator of the purchasing power of a currency. Hence, the non-ICP method of using the exchange rate to convert income denominated in domestic currency to a numeraire currency (usually the US dollar) tends to exaggerate the dispersion of per capita incomes by systematically understating those of poorer countries.

Kravis further states that the ICP method also enables the comparison of *price levels* between countries, and not just the *relative changes* in them. He shows that we are actually able to compare the German price levels in the 1980s with those of the USA, instead of just observing changes in German prices relative to US prices. The third advantage of the ICP method is that it allows comparison of the relative quantities and prices of goods that make up the GDPs of different countries. For instance, exchange rate deviation from PPP varies for different goods; that is, the relative price structures of countries differ. This means that inter-country quantity relationships which make up GDP may not be consistent with what exchange rate conversions make them out to be. With the ICP method, however, we are able to deduce whether a country's spending share is higher than another's because of its ability to absorb a particular good or merely because its prices are higher.

The ICP method is not without its critics, however. The reason that exchange rates continue to be used, instead of the purportedly superior PPPs, is that the ICP has several methodological problems. One objection is the use of world average prices to value the GDP components (Isenman, 1980). The argument here is that since world average prices are dominated by the larger weights of rich countries, price weights that are not reflective of the low-income countries tend to push up their relative quantity indices. Another area of contention is the ICP treatment of 'comparison-resistant' services, which have no identifiable unit of output which could be easily priced. Maddison's (1983) objection to the use of the ICP stems from the significant differences between his estimates of real GDP per capita for developing countries and those extrapolated from ICP results, which he attributes to the difference in treatment of the services component. Rogoff (1996) argues that ICP data are only gathered at five-year intervals (beginning in 1970) and country coverage is limited, which means that data from non-benchmark years and countries must be obtained by extrapolation. Moreover, there is also a long time lag between collection of the data and its availability. These problems notwithstanding, Kravis supports the use of PPPs over exchange rates since 'methodological improvements can and doubtless will be made, but the indices of real per capita GDP are little changed by the use of alternative methods' (p. 23).

Bahmani-Oskooee (1992) tests for the validity of the PBH as a long-run phenomenon using cointegration techniques. He claims that the problem of using the actual rate as proxy for the EER could be partly resolved in this context, since the actual exchange rate would tend to the equilibrium rate over the longer term. He is also able to avoid the issue of using PPP versus the exchange rate to convert income from domestic to standard currency by using productivity indices which are unit-free. This measure is calculated as the number of units of each country's currency per man-hour and reported in index form. Of the six countries tested, he concludes that a long-run relationship exists between productivity and the deviation of PPP from the EER, even though he fails to find such a relationship for one other country, while claiming that the data for the remaining two are not 'suitable' for the method used.

De Gregorio *et al.* (1994) use time-series and cross-sectional data to determine the cause of differentials in sectoral inflation, as defined by the behaviour of the relative price of N (in terms of T). They demonstrate that the relative price of N is determined solely by technological conditions; that is, there exists a positive relationship between increased productivity growth in the T sector and the relative price of N, as stated by the PBH.

Further qualifications to PPP

Officer (1976a) categorizes the limitations of PPP theory into four groups: namely, the *index-number problem* relating to price parity, *absolute price parity, relative price parity* and *cost parity*. The *index-number problem*, discussed earlier, pertains to the method of calculating the parity condition. Given that the individual prices used in PPP computations are assumed to represent free-market transactions, the existence of effective rationing and price controls in either country would not be truly reflective of each country's buying power. Furthermore, since the price indices comprise only a sample of commodities, any computed price parity is not truly representative of the true theoretical parity (Pigou, 1922). Another point of contention is centred on the composite index itself; that is, the incorporation of N as well as T, as against the use of T prices only.

Within the context of *absolute price parity*, Officer suggests that the existence of market imperfections such as tariffs and transportation costs could result in deviations in the short-run EER from PPP, to the extent that the former bears practically no relationship to the latter because the price responsiveness of T is greatly reduced. This theory is later supported by Miller (1984) who finds that intra-European PPP relationships perform better than transatlantic ones. He attributes these results to the lower transport costs within Europe, and the tariff and EMS implications as a result of EEC cooperation. These problems are augmented when controls are extended to the domestic sector in the form of price and wage controls, among others. Other criticisms of absolute PPP look at the roles played by income (Yeager, 1958, 1976), long-term capital flows (Houthakker, 1962; Officer, 1974) and causation between exchange rates and prices (Balassa, 1964; Keynes, 1923).

Michael *et al.* (1994a) offer other explanations for departures from PPP. They examine the roles played by transportation and transaction costs in long- and short-run PPP, respectively, taking into account the non-stationarity characteristic of price series. They exploit this feature by using the cointegration model for their analysis. Their results show that long-run PPP is comfortably satisfied when transportation costs are taken into consideration. Furthermore, they are able to conclude that short-run deviations from PPP, while statistically predictable, cannot be systematically exploited for arbitrage gains since the vast majority of forecasts fall within the transaction cost bands.

In a subsequent paper, Michael *et al.* (1994b, p. 2) argue that

> conventional tests of cointegration between exchange rates and prices may be seriously biased towards rejection of the hypothesis of PPP in the presence of transactions bands [since] the existence of transactions costs will imply a non-linear response to deviations from purchasing power parity which can be represented as a non-linear error correcting process [which] is in contrast with the linear framework in standard cointegration analysis.

Using monthly data for the interwar period and annual data spanning two centuries on non-linear 'threshold models', they find evidence of non-linear adjustment to PPP deviations in the presence of transaction bands – that is, no adjustment within the transactions band but quite fast adjustment outside the band – to which they attribute the mixed results in previous studies of PPP.

One of the main problems of calculating *relative price parity* is the need for a base period where the exchange rate is in long-run equilibrium. However, this is possible only if the exchange rate is freely floating at the time; otherwise there is no guarantee that it is even in short-run equilibrium. Furthermore, even if a free float exists, its value may have been affected by temporary factors, such as short-term capital flows, that would cause it to move away from the long-run equilibrium.[8] Given the difficulty in locating an equilibrium base period, Bacha and Taylor (1971) and Bunting (1939) argue that the theory is practically unusable.

Another criticism of relative price parity concentrates on the possibility that economic conditions, either structural or non-structural in nature, may have changed since the base period. Non-structural changes include the magnitude of trade restrictions and transportation costs, and conditions governing international capital flows and investment income. Changes in tastes, technology, factor supplies and market form are classified as structural changes, which affect 'the shape or position of the economy's reciprocal demand curve for foreign commodities with respect to their (real) price denominated in domestic commodities' (Officer, 1982, p. 130). Thus, Bunting (1939) posits that the base period should be as close as possible to the current period when computing relative PPP, to minimize the scope for structural changes.

The structural change considered most damaging to PPP is that which involves a differential shift in the T/N price ratio as between countries (Officer, 1982). This is the PBH discussed above. Balassa's (1964) argument of non-uniform productivity advantage – that is, greater for T than for N – enjoyed by the richer country results in a bias in *absolute* PPP. The corresponding bias to *relative* PPP occurs when there is an increase (decrease) over time in the richer country's productivity advantage, as measured by a higher (lower) rate of growth in per capita income, compared to the poorer country.

Harris (1936), who first criticized the *cost parity* concept, contends that the inconsistencies of cost components across countries make comparison difficult. Tamagna (1945), in turn, argues that the comparison of wages across countries at different stages of development would be difficult because of diverse output composition and changes in productivity. The problem of data availability leads Artus (1978, p. 287) to observe that the 'prices of intermediate inputs and capital services are practically always ignored'.

Using the *asset market theory* of exchange rate determination, Frenkel (1981) addresses the question of whether exchange rates and national price levels are comparable, given the intrinsic differences between the two. This theory is based on the notion that the exchange rate, being the relative price of two durable assets (currencies), should be analysed within the same framework as that of other asset prices. In an efficient and organized market for durable assets, new information about the future is immediately incorporated into current prices, thus precluding arbitrage opportunities. It follows then that during periods dominated by 'news', asset prices would exhibit relatively higher levels of variability. Similarly, we would expect greater volatility in exchange rates during such periods. By contrast, it is well-documented that aggregate price indices, which reflect the prices of less durable goods and services, are less sensitive to news which alters future expectations. Broadly speaking, exchange rates reflect *future* expectations, while prices are an indication of *present* and *past* circumstances which are reflected in existing contracts.

The 'stickiness' exhibited by prices, compared to the quickness of the currency market in responding to new information, implies that exchange rate fluctuations would not be matched by corresponding fluctuations of aggregate price levels, at least in the short term. This behaviour is demonstrated by persistent departures from PPP in the 1970s as a result of real shocks to the world economy in the form of oil embargos, supply shocks, commodity booms and shortages, changes in demand for money supply and differential productivity growth, as well as political uncertainty. It is also consistent with Frenkel's (1978) findings on causality between prices and exchange rates. In that paper, his results indicate that prices do not 'cause' exchange rates, rather, that exchange rates 'cause' prices. He surmises that 'this pattern of "causality" is consistent with the hypothesis that speeds of adjustment in asset markets exceed those in the commodity markets' (p. 183).

It has often been held that the failure of the law of one price is due, in large part, to systematic attempts by firms operating in international markets to stabilise destination market prices, when nominal exchange rates change, in order to protect market share. Ghosh and Wolf (1994) distinguish between deliberate pricing-to-market behaviour and inadvertent import-currency price stabilization stemming from menu costs, in trying to explain observed departures from PPP. Firms are said to 'price to market' when they charge different local prices across export markets to reflect the particular local competitive situation. Any exchange rate movement is absorbed by altering the home currency export price. Menu costs consist of two components: informational costs which capture the inconvenience to customers as prices are changed, resulting in possible lost sales, and administrative costs which are incurred when determining and implementing new prices. The authors argue that the speed of adjustment of the real exchange rate to nominal exchange rate movements is determined by the pricing behaviour of such firms. The cover prices of *The Economist* magazine are considered suitable data for this analysis as the journal is a single homogenous product sold in a large number of countries, whose limited life precludes international arbitrage opportunities. Furthermore, the aggregation problems associated with the common use of composite indices – such as the indistinguishability between the two types of pricing behaviour – are avoided here. Based on the significance of lagged exchange rate changes on cross-country relative price changes, Ghosh and Wolf conclude that they are unable to reject the possibility that menu costs, rather than pricing-to-market behaviour, are responsible for the observed departures from parity.

Bearing in mind our earlier discussion on the limitations of PPP imposed by the PBH, Krugman's (1990b) *perfect integration hypothesis* states that the globalization of world markets, *via* improved telecommunication and transportation, has enabled international arbitrage to the extent that cross-border economic transactions can be considered to take place within one global marketplace. As such, national price levels are seen to diverge only through exchange rate changes which result in differential inflation, rather than due to any changes in relative prices. This appears at odds with the PBH assumption that the exchange rate between two countries is determined by the relative prices of T between them. Furthermore, Krugman's finding that exchange rate changes are not passed through, even to the prices of T, implies that there may be factors other than those presumed in these two hypotheses that cause deviations in the PPP. He concludes that 'we still live in a world of highly imperfectly integrated markets, and one in which…there is still quite a lot of price stickiness denominated in domestic currency' (p. 97).

Rogers and Jenkins (1995) categorize theories that explain departures from PPP into those that focus on the properties of price levels and those that concentrate on nominal exchange rate determination in a world of sticky prices. The former is the PBH as discussed earlier, while the latter posits that the nominal exchange rate responds to shocks in the financial assets market and, because of price stickiness, changes in the nominal exchange rate are *real* changes. Using disaggregated price data from 11 OECD countries, the authors examine the roles played by 'haircuts', that is, the presence of N in the general price index, and 'hysteresis', which is defined as sluggishness in firms' pricing policies with respect to exchange rate changes. Their analysis suggests that both these factors play a part in explaining the empirical failure of PPP. For instance, they find a high correlation between the common-currency price of food across borders and the real exchange rate, implying that sticky prices are a predominant cause of deviations of PPP. They also find that the results of the cointegration and unit root tests provide 'mild support for the Samuelson–Balassa class of models' (p. 353).

In a similar vein, Engel and Rogers (1996) find that physical distance plays an important role in explaining the failure of PPP between two locations. Furthermore, the variability in price ratios for similar goods is also affected by crossing the border between two countries. Using disaggregated CPI data from 23 major cities in the US and Canada over the June 1978 to June 1993 period, they show that 'crossing the border' is equivalent to adding 7182 miles between two cities in the same country.

The authors offer three possible explanations as to why the border may matter. First, the consumer goods could be subject to sticky prices in terms of the currency of the country in which they are sold. The highly variable nominal exchange rate means that cross-border relative prices would fluctuate along with the exchange rate, but the country relative prices would be relatively stable.[9] Secondly, the inter-country variation in prices could reflect variation in the costs of N, such as marketing services, that are required in selling the goods. To the extent that the movement of labour across borders is more restricted than that within a country, one would expect more variation in cross-border prices than within-country prices. Finally, there are the direct costs such as tariffs and trade restrictions. Given the relatively low trade barriers between the US and Canada, especially since the Canadian–US Free Trade Agreement was effected in January 1990, Engel and Rogers posit that trade restrictions cannot account for all the cross-border relative price variability in their results. However, they are unable to conclude whether segmented labour markets or sticky nominal prices are responsible for the significance of the cross-border variable.

Summary

PPP as a theory of exchange rate determination is probably the most useful and used of all exchange rate theories, despite its many detractors. It is relatively simple and intuitively appealing – its basic ingredients are minimal, that is, prices at home and abroad, and the rate of exchange between two countries; and it has important implications for economic policy decisions. Furthermore, the ability of the theory to allow for adjustments and extensions when taking into account limiting factors further contributes to its versatility. This is evidenced by the surge in the number of publications on PPP research over the past decade alone, as we will discuss in Chapter 2.

Although a plethora of studies already exists on PPP, it is generally accepted that empirical work on the topic could still be improved. Issues such as the choice of an optimal equilibrium exchange rate and an appropriate price index, as well as biases imposed by productivity differentials, are paramount in ensuring the validity of any results obtained. In this book, we will attempt to incorporate these factors into our tests and analyses of PPP.

Notes

1. See, for example, Wheatley (1803, 1807, 1819) and Ricardo (1810/11, 1811a, 1811b, 1811c). The origins of PPP theory are analyzed in detail by Frenkel (1976) and Officer (1982).
2. See, for example, Cassel (1916a, 1916b, 1921, 1922, 1926, 1928, 1932).
3. Studies by Adler and Lehmann (1983), Huizinga (1987) and Meese and Rogoff (1988) are unable to reject the hypothesis that real exchange rates follow a random walk under the floating exchange rate regime. However, recent studies by Abuaf and Jorion (1990), Diebold, Husted and Rush (1991) and Lothian (1990) find evidence of mean-reverting behaviour in real exchange rates, using long-term time series data (see Chapter 2 for a more detailed discussion). Other research into real exchange rate behaviour during the float include Dornbusch (1987), Frenkel and Meese (1987), Meese (1990) and Officer (1976a). Surveys of the literature in this area are provided by Dornbusch (1987), Lothian (1997), Officer (1976a), Rogoff (1996) and Taylor (1995).
4. See Saidi and Swoboda (1983) for a more detailed explanation.

5. Note that Cassel's (1926) concept of the EER is slightly different in that it specifically requires equilibrium in the *current* account of the balance of payments.
6. The mechanics of this concept are discussed in further detail in Chapter 3 (pp. 72–3).
7. For example, low-income countries are labour-abundant and since services are labour-intensive they would be relatively cheaper in low-income countries compared to high-income ones.
8. In the course of his research, Cassel provides numerous reasons as to why floating exchange rates may systematically diverge from PPP. Summaries are provided by Angell (1925), Bunting (1939), Holmes (1967), Myhrman (1976), Officer (1982) and Sadie (1948).
9. See previous study by Mussa (1986) on the effect of sticky prices on the variance of the real exchange rate.

References

Abuaf, N. and P. Jorion (1990) 'Purchasing Power Parity in the Long Run', *Journal of Finance*, vol. 45, pp. 157–74.

Adler, M. and B. Dumas (1983) 'International Portfolio Choice and Corporation Finance: A Synthesis', *Journal of Finance*, vol. 38, pp. 925–84.

Adler, M. and B. Lehmann (1983) 'Deviations from Purchasing Power Parity in the Long Run', *Journal of Finance*, vol. 38, pp. 1471–87.

Angell, J. W. (1925) 'Monetary Theory and Monetary Policy: Some Recent Discussions', *Quarterly Journal of Economics*, vol. 39, pp. 267–99.

Artus, J. R. (1978) 'Methods of Assessing the Long-run Equilibrium Value of an Exchange Rate', *Journal of International Economics*, vol. 8, pp. 277–99.

Bacha, E. and L. Taylor (1971) 'Foreign Exchange Shadow Prices: A Critical Review of Current Theories', *Quarterly Journal of Economics*, vol. 85, pp. 197–224.

Bahmani-Oskooee, M. (1992) 'A Time-Series Approach to Test the Productivity Bias Hypothesis in Purchasing Power Parity', *Kyklos*, vol. 45, pp. 227–36.

Balassa, B. (1964) 'The Purchasing-Power Parity Doctrine: A Reappraisal', *Journal of Political Economy*, vol. 72, pp. 584–96.

Bartolini, L. (1995) 'Purchasing Power Parity Measures of Competitiveness', *Finance and Development*, September, pp. 46–9.

Betton, S., M. D. Levi and R. Uppal (1995) 'Index-Induced Errors and Purchasing Power Parity: Bounding the Possible Bias', *Journal of International Financial Markets, Institutions and Money*, vol. 5, pp. 165–79.

Bunting, F. H. (1939) 'The Purchasing Power Parity Theory Re-Examined', *Southern Economic Journal*, vol. 5, pp. 282–301.

Cassel, G. (1916a) 'The Present Situation of the Foreign Exchanges', *Economic Journal*, vol. 26, pp. 62–5.

Cassel, G. (1916b) 'The Present Situation of the Foreign Exchanges', *Economic Journal*, vol. 26, pp. 319–23.

Cassel, G. (1921) *The World's Monetary Problems*. London: Constable.

Cassel, G. (1922) *Money and Foreign Exchange After 1914*. London: Constable.

Cassel, G. (1926) 'Exchanges, Foreign', *Encyclopedia Britannica*, Supplementary Vol. 1, 13th edn, pp. 1086–9.

Cassel, G. (1928) 'The International Movements of Capital', in *Foreign Investments*, pp. 1–93. Chicago: University of Chicago Press.

Cassel, G. (1932) *The Theory of Social Economy*, rev edn. New York: Harcourt Brace.

Clague, C. and V. Tanzi (1972) 'Human Capital, Natural Resources and the Purchasing-Power Parity Doctrine: Some Empirical Results', *Economia Internazionale*, vol. 25, pp. 3–18.

Clements, K. W. and M. Semudram (1983) 'An International Comparison of the Price of Nontraded Goods', *Weltwirtschaftliches Archiv*, vol. 119, pp. 356–63.

De Gregorio, J., A. Giovannini and H.C. Wolf (1994) 'International Evidence on Tradeables and Nontradeables Inflation', *European Economic Review*, vol. 38, pp. 1225–44.

de Vries, M. G. (1968) 'Exchange Depreciation in Developing Countries', *IMF Staff Papers*, no. 15, pp. 560–78.

Diebold, F. X., S. Husted and M. Rush (1991) 'Real Exchange Rates under the Gold Standard', *Journal of Political Economy*, vol. 99, pp. 1252–71.

Dornbusch, R. (1976) 'Expectations and Exchange Rate Dynamics', *Journal of Political Economy*, vol. 84, pp. 1161–76.

Dornbusch, R. (1987) 'Purchasing Power Parity', in *The New Palgrave: A Dictionary of Economics*, eds J. Eatwell, M. Milgate and P. Newman, pp. 1075–85. London: Palgrave Macmillan.

Edwards, S. (1989) *Real Exchange Rate, Devaluation and Adjustment*. Cambridge: MIT Press.

Engel, C. and J.H. Rogers (1996) 'How Wide is the Border?', *American Economic Review*, vol. 86, pp. 1112–25.

Frankel, J. A. (1985) 'Six Possible Meanings of "Overvaluation": The 1981–85 Dollar', *Essays in International Finance*, no. 159. Princeton: Princeton University Press.

Frankel, J. A. (1994) 'Introduction', in *The Internationalization of Equity Markets*, pp. 1–20. Chicago: University of Chicago Press.

Frankel, J. A. and R. Meese (1987) 'Are Exchange Rages Excessively Variable?', in *NBER Macroeconomics Annual*, ed. Stanley Fischer, pp. 117–53. Cambridge: MIT Press.

Frenkel, J. A. (1976) 'A Monetary Approach to the Exchange Rate: Doctrinal Aspects and Empirical Evidence', *Scandinavian Journal of Economics*, vol. 78, pp. 200–24.

Frenkel, J. A. (1978) 'Purchasing Power Parity: Doctrinal Perspective and Evidence from the 1920s', *Journal of International Economics*, vol. 8, pp. 169–91.

Frenkel, J. A. (1981) 'The Collapse of Purchasing Power Parities during the 1970s', *European Economic Review*, vol. 16, pp. 145–65.

Frenkel, J. A. and M. L. Mussa (1980) 'The Efficiency of Foreign Exchange Markets and Measures of Turbulence', *American Economic Review*, vol. 70, pp. 374–81.

Froot, K. A. and K. Rogoff (1995) 'Perspectives on PPP and Long-Run Real Exchange Rates', in *Handbook of International Economics*, eds G. Grossman and K. Rogoff, vol. 3, pp. 1647–88. Amsterdam: North-Holland Press.

Ghosh, A. R. and H. C. Wolf (1994) 'Pricing in International Markets: Lessons from *The Economist*'. NBER Working Paper Series, no. 4806, National Bureau of Economic Research, Cambridge, Massachusetts.

Goldstein, M. and L. H. Officer (1979) 'New Measures of Prices and Productivity for Tradeable and Nontradeable Goods', *The Review of Income and Wealth*, vol. 25, pp. 413–27.

Hagen, E. E. (1957) 'Comment', in *Problems in the International Comparison of Economic Accounts*, pp. 377–88. Princeton: Princeton University Press.

Harris, S. E. (1936) 'Measures of Currency Overvaluation and Stabilization', *Explorations in Economics*, pp. 35–45. New York: McGraw-Hill.

Harrod, R. F. (1939) *International Economics*. Cambridge: Nisbet & Co.

Holmes, J. M. (1967) 'The Purchasing-Power-Parity Theory: In Defence of Gustav Cassel as a Modern Theorist', *Journal of Political Economy*, vol. 75, pp. 686–95.

Houthakker, H. S. (1962) 'Exchange Rate Adjustment', in *Factors Affecting the United States Balance of Payments*, pp. 287–304, Compilation of studies prepared for the Subcommittee on International Exchange Payments, Joint Economic Committee, 87th Congress, 2nd Session. Washington, DC: US Government Printing Office.

Huizinga, J. (1987) 'An Empirical Investigation of the Long-Run Behavior of Real Exchange Rates', *Carnegie–Rochester Series on Public Policy*, vol. 27, pp. 149–215.

Isenman, P. (1980) 'Inter-Country Comparison of "Real" (PPP) Incomes: Revised Estimates and Unresolved Questions', *World Development*, vol. 8, pp. 61–72.

Keynes, J. M. (1923) *A Tract on Monetary Reform*. London: Palgrave Macmillan.

Keynes, J. M. (1930) *A Treatise on Money*, vol. 1. London: Palgrave Macmillan.

Kravis, I. B. (1986) 'The Three Faces of the International Comparison Project', *Research Observer*, vol. 1, pp. 3–26.

Kravis, I. B., A. W. Heston and R. Summers (1978) in collaboration with A. Civitello, *International Comparisons of Real Product and Purchasing Power*. Baltimore: Johns Hopkins Press.

Kravis, I. B. and R. Lipsey (1978) 'Price Behavior in the Light of Balance of Payments Theories', *Journal of International Economics*, vol. 8, pp. 193–247.

Kravis, I. B., Z. Kennessey, A. W. Heston and R. Summers (1975) *A System of International Comparisons of Gross Products and Purchasing Power*. Baltimore: Johns Hopkins Press.

Krugman, P. R. (1990a) 'Equilibrium Exchange Rates', in *International Policy Coordination and Exchange Rate Fluctuations*, eds W. H. Branson, J. A. Frenkel and M. Goldstein, pp. 159–95. Chicago: University of Chicago Press.

Krugman, P. R. (1990b) 'Hindsight on the Strong Dollar', in *The Economics of the Dollar Cycle*, eds S. Gerlach and P. A. Petri, pp. 82–118. Cambridge: MIT Press.

Lothian, J. R. (1990) 'A Century Plus of Japanese Exchange Rate Behavior', *Japan and the World Economy*, vol. 2, pp. 47–70.

Lothian, J. R. (1997) 'Multi-Country Evidence on the Behavior of Purchasing Power Parity under the Current Float', *Journal of International Money and Finance*, vol. 16, pp. 19–35.

Maddison, A. (1983) 'A Comparison of the Levels of GDP per Capita in Developed and Developing Countries, 1790–1980', *Journal of Economic History*, vol. 43, pp. 27–41.

Manzur, M. (1990) 'An International Comparison of Prices and Exchange Rates: A New Test of Purchasing Power Parity', *Journal of International Money and Finance*, vol. 9, pp. 75–91.

Meese, R. (1990) 'Currency Fluctuations in the Post-Bretton Woods Period', *Journal of Economic Perspectives*, vol. 4, pp. 117–34.

Meese, R. and K. Rogoff (1988) 'Was It Real? The Exchange Rate Interest Differential Relation Over the Modern Floating Exchange Rate Period', *Journal of Finance*, vol. 43, pp. 933–48.

Michael, P., A. R. Nobay and D. Peel (1994a) 'Purchasing Power Parity Yet Again: Evidence from Spatially Separated Commodity Markets', *Journal of International Money and Finance*, vol. 13, pp. 637–57.

Michael, P., A. R. Nobay and D. Peel (1994b) 'Exchange Rates, Transactions Bands and Cassell's Doctrine of PPP', *Liverpool Research Papers in Economics and Finance*, no. 9403, Department of Economics and Accounting, University of Liverpool.

Miller, S. (1984) 'Purchasing Power Parity and Relative Price Variability', *European Economic Review*, vol. 26, pp. 353–67.

Mussa, M. L. (1986) 'Nominal Exchange Rate Regimes and the Behaviour of Real Exchange Rates: Evidence and Implications', *Carnegie–Rochester Conference Series on Public Policy*, vol. 25, pp. 117–214.

Myhrman, J. (1976) 'Experiences of Flexible Exchange Rates in Earlier Periods: Theories, Evidence and a New View', *Scandinavian Journal of Economics*, vol. 78, pp. 169–96.

Officer, L. H. (1974) 'Purchasing Power Parity and Factor Price Equalization', *Kyklos*, vol. 27, pp. 868–78.

Officer, L. H. (1976a) 'The Purchasing-Power-Parity Theory of Exchange Rates: A Review Article', *IMF Staff Papers*, no. 23, pp. 1–60.

Officer, L. H. (1976b) 'The Productivity Bias in Purchasing Power Parity: An Econometric Investigation', *IMF Staff Papers*, no. 23, pp. 545–79.

Officer, L. H. (1982) 'Purchasing Power Parity and Exchange Rates: Theory, Evidence and Relevance', in *Contemporary Studies in Economic and Financial Analysis*, eds E. I. Altman and I. Walter, vol. 35. Connecticut: JAI Press.

Pick, D. H. and T. L. Volrath (1994) 'Real Exchange Rate Misalignment and Agricultural Export Performance in Developing Countries', in *Economic Development and Cultural Change*, pp. 555–71. Chicago: University of Chicago Press.

Pigou, A. C. (1922) 'The Foreign Exchanges', *Quarterly Journal of Economics*, vol. 37, pp. 52–74.

Ricardo, D. (1810/11) *The High Price of Bullion*, reprinted in Sraffa (1951), vol. III, pp. 47–127.

Ricardo, D. (1811a) *Reply to Mr. Bosanquet's Practical Observations on the Report of the Bullion Committee*, reprinted in Sraffa (1951), vol. III, pp. 157–256.

Ricardo, D. (1811b) *Letter to [Malthus?], 23rd June 1811*, reprinted in Sraffa (1952), vol. VI, pp. 29–30.

Ricardo, D. (1811c) *Letter to Malthus, 17 July 1811*, reprinted in Sraffa (1952), vol. VI, pp. 25–40.

Rogers, J. H. (1995) 'Real Shocks and Real Exchange Rates in Really Long-Term Data', International Finance Discussion Papers, no. 493, Board of Governors of the Federal Reserve System, Washington DC.

Rogers, J. H. and M. Jenkins (1995) 'Haircuts or Hysteresis? Sources of Movements in Real Exchange Rates', *Journal of International Economics*, vol. 38, pp. 339–60.

Rogoff, K. (1996) 'The Purchasing Power Parity Puzzle', *Journal of Economic Literature*, vol. 34, pp. 647–68.

Rothschild, K. (1958) 'Actual and Implied Exchange Rates', *Scottish Journal of Political Economy*, vol. 5, pp. 229–35.

Sadie, J. L. (1948) 'Further Observations on Foreign Exchange Rates', *South African Journal of Economics*, vol. 16, pp. 194–201.

Saidi, N. and A. Swoboda (1983) 'Nominal and Real Exchange Rates: Issues and Some Evidence', in *Recent Issues in the Theory of Flexible Exchange Rates*, eds E. Claassen and P. Salin, pp. 3–27. Amsterdam: North-Holland Press.

Samuelson, P. A. (1964) 'Theoretical Notes on Trade Problems', *Review of Economics and Statistics*, vol. 46, pp. 145–54.

Sjaastad, L. (1991) *PPP and the Real Exchange Rate: The Swiss Case*, Discussion Paper no. 91-24, Department of Economics, University of Western Australia.

Sraffa, P. (with M. H. Dobb) *The Works and Correspondences of David Ricardo* (1950–). Cambridge: Cambridge University Press.

Stockman, A. C. (1987) 'The Equilibrium Approach to Exchange Rates', *Federal Reserve Bank of Richmond Economic Review*, March, 12–31.

Stockman, A. C. (1988) 'Real Exchange Rate Variability Under Pegged and Floating Nominal Exchange Rate Systems: An Equilibrium Theory', *Carnegie–Rochester Conference Series on Public Policy*, vol. 29, pp. 259–94.

Tamagna, F. M. (1945) 'The Fixing of Foreign Exchange Rates', *Journal of Political Economy*, vol. 53, pp. 57–72.

Taylor, M. P. (1995) 'The Economics of Exchange Rates', *Journal of Economic Literature*, vol. 33, pp. 13–47.

Voltaire, K. and E. J. Stack (1980) 'A Divisia Version of the Country-Product-Dummy Method', *Economics Letters*, vol. 5, pp. 97–9.

Wheatley, J. (1803) *Remarks on Currency and Commerce*. London: Cadell & Davies.

Wheatley, J. (1807) *An Essay on the Theory of Money and Principles of Commerce*. London: Cadell & Davies.

Wheatley, J. (1819) *Report on the Reports of the Bank Committees*. London: Longman, Hurst, Rees, Orme & Brown.

Williamson, J. (1983) *The Exchange Rate System*. Cambridge: MIT Press.

Yeager, L. B. (1958) 'A Rehabilitation of Purchasing-Power Parity', *Journal of Political Economy*, vol. 66, pp. 516–30.

Yeager, L. B. (1976) *International Monetary Relations: Theory, History, and Policy*. New York: Harper & Row.

2
The Growing Evidence on Purchasing Power Parity

Co-authored with Yihui Lan

> The evidence that ... [price] adjusted real exchange rates ... are apparently mean reverting over the floating rate period is ... an important finding ... corroborating other recently emerging evidence that long-run PPP may hold after all. Indeed, it seems that the profession's confidence in long-run PPP, having been low for a number of years, may itself be mean reverting.
>
> (Mark P. Taylor and Lucio Sarno, 1998, p. 308)

The explosion of research on the topic of purchasing power parity (PPP) since the 1970s is testimony to the theory's undoubted appeal as a method for exchange rate determination. Indeed, the concept of PPP has endured some controversial findings in the empirical literature to become even more popular over the past decade, as the use of more sophisticated econometric techniques has evolved. Notably, the application of unit root and cointegration tests dominated the literature during the 1990s, with the majority of studies finding support for PPP for both developed and developing countries. However, doubts about the 'power' of these tests have given rise to debate over the veracity of using time-series data versus cross-sectional, or panel, data. Meanwhile, *The Economist*'s Big Mac Index has been another catalyst for PPP research over the past decade, with its easy accessibility and international appeal. Empirical tests of exchange rate behaviour, using the Index, have been surprisingly successful in proving the PPP condition, and have encouraged a school of research using this metric.

Introduction

Although the theory of PPP was resurrected by Gustav Cassel in the 1920s – centuries after its birth in the 1500s – rigorous empirical examination of the theory only first appeared in the 1960s.[1] However, it was the collapse of the Bretton Woods system and the move to flexible exchange rates in the early-1970s that ignited the huge surge in interest in the ensuing years. At the time, however, the high volatility in exchange rates, in both nominal and real terms, almost rendered the PPP concept untenable.[2] Flood (1981) and Mussa (1982) argue that since domestic and foreign goods are imperfect substitutes, the real exchange rate must adjust to real shocks, requiring divergent movements between the exchange rate and domestic and foreign price levels. Dornbush (1976) had previously offered an intuitively attractive explanation for observed short-term departures from long-term monetary equilibrium – that exchange rates tend to 'overshoot', given domestic price rigidities.[3]

Perhaps it is testimony to the appealing simplicity of the PPP theory that it continues to fascinate and challenge researchers several centuries after the Spanish scholars gave birth to the idea. If anything, interest in the doctrine has exploded in recent times, even compared to the immediate post-Bretton Woods period. Clearly, PPP has endured as a fundamental building block in models of exchange rate determination, despite its ups and downs in the empirical literature over time.

In this chapter, we will review and compare the 'trends' in PPP literature, notably, the evolution of research methods used and the empirical findings in the post-Bretton Woods period. In particular, we focus on the evidence of the last decade, with the findings during this period suggesting that, on balance, PPP holds over the longer term across industrial and developing countries. The chapter is organized as follows. First, we look at the increasing popularity of PPP research over the years, and the different research methods used over time. This is followed by a review of the evidence in the 1990s, after which we consider the role played by *The Economist*'s Big Mac Index in helping to repopularize the PPP concept. We conclude with a summary.

The 'trends' in PPP research

The interest in PPP research has grown at a very rapid clip over the past three decades. As a quick test of its popularity, a keyword search was carried out in *EconLit* for the term 'purchasing power parity' or 'PPP', along with several other oft-researched areas in economics such as 'inflation', 'unemployment', 'interest rate', 'exchange rate', and 'foreign direct investment' (FDI). Figure 2.1 shows that although the *absolute* number of research papers produced on PPP has trailed publications in the other topics, interest in PPP has grown at a relatively quicker *rate* over time. Notably, research publications on PPP have grown at an average annual rate of 18 per cent since the 1970s, second only to the increasingly popular FDI, which has grown at an average annual rate of almost 21 per cent during the same period.[4]

Not surprisingly, the wealth of research on PPP has yielded a mixture of results over the years, which has thoroughly vexed proponents of the theory. Although issues such as the index-number problem, the productivity bias hypothesis, the determination of the equilibrium exchange rate and other caveats – as discussed in Chapter 1 – have been credited as causes for observed deviations from parity, the choice

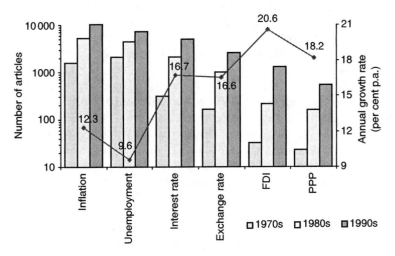

Figure 2.1   The growth of economic research
Source: Lan (2002).

of research method and data sample period also appears to play an important role in the determination of PPP. Since different research methods have been 'in vogue' during different periods, this may explain the ebb and flow in confidence in PPP as a tool for exchange rate determination, over time.

Prior to the mid-1980s, empirical tests were largely concerned with simple specifications of PPP which centred on coefficient restrictions using ordinary least squares (OLS) and generalized least squares (GLS). These methods tend to reject PPP strongly, except for hyperinflation countries.[5] However, it is now widely accepted that such straight-forward tests of PPP, which Froot and Rogoff (1995) term the 'stage-one tests', take no account of non-stationarity of relative prices and exchange rates, and thus produce possibly spurious results.

In the second-half of the 1980s, many PPP studies focused on testing the efficient market hypothesis on real exchange rates, but could not reject the null of a random walk (Adler and Lehmann, 1983; Mark, 1990; Meese and Rogoff, 1988). Moreover, researchers failed to show cointegration between nominal exchange rates and relative prices (Corbae and Ouliaris, 1988; Enders, 1988; Patel, 1990). The negative results have since been attributed largely to the low power of statistical tests of non-stationarity, rather than that PPP does not hold (Abuaf and Jorion, 1990; Edison *et al.*, 1997; Frankel, 1986, 1990; Johnson, 1993).

It is argued that the long-run nature of PPP[6] means that a sufficient data sample is crucial in determining the empirical validity of the theory. Froot and Rogoff (1995, p. 1648) observe that '... the advent of floating exchange rates made it obvious ... that PPP is not a short-run relationship; price level movements do not begin to offset exchange rate swings on a monthly or even annual basis'. They fur-ther suggest that the 'phenomenal volatility of floating exchange rates' (p. 1653) makes it very difficult to distinguish between slow mean reversion and a random walk real exchange rate, 'especially if one relies only on post-Bretton Woods data'.

The long-run PPP relationship is also very evident from research into the 'half-lives' of deviations from parity; that is, the time it takes for real exchange rate innovations to diminish to half their size. Figure 2.2 summarizes the findings from various studies into half-lives, from recent PPP literature. Based on this sample, the majority of estimates lie between 3 and 5 years; the mean of half-lives is 4.1 years, which is consistent with the 'long run', as reported in the survey by Froot and

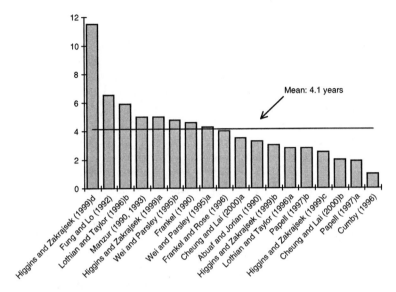

Figure 2.2   Estimates of PPP half-lives

Note: Where a study contains more than one estimate of half-life, the estimates are distinguished by the alphabets 'a', 'b', etc.

Source: Lan (2002).

Rogoff (1995). Lothian and Taylor (1996) find that first-order autoregressive models, estimated on pre-float data, perform very well during the floating period compared to alternative random walk models. This forecasting superiority increases with the time horizon of data used, thus providing support for the slow mean-reversion nature of real exchange rates. They argue that the slow adjustment, plus the low power of conventional unit root tests where data are insufficient, account for the observed failure of such tests for the float period.

Not surprisingly, then, the relatively short time-period of the post-Bretton Woods era is sometimes seen as a stumbling block to obtaining more reliable results.[7] Researchers have consequently attempted to circumvent this problem by using (1) longer periods of data; and (2) cross-country time-series analyses, or 'panel-data' techniques.[8]

While long-horizon data studies have almost invariably provided evidence in favour of PPP (Abuaf and Jorion, 1990; Cheung and Lai, 1994; Diebold *et al.*, 1991; Glen, 1992; Kuo and Mikkola, 1999; Lothian and Taylor, 1996; Parkes and Savvides, 1999), several flaws in the approach have been noted. Namely, the use of real exchange rates over long historical periods means that the data are vulnerable to significant 'noise' such as periods of war and natural disasters.[9] Another caveat is that these datasets comprise a mix of fixed and floating rates which could skew the results.[10] Moreover, since data are available over long time spans largely for industrial countries, the favourable results may be exaggerated by the 'survivorship bias' problem, raised by Froot and Rogoff (1995). Using long-horizon time-series data, Engel and Kim (1999) and Engel (2000) confirm the existence of large-size bias in tests of PPP.

Thus, the use of panel data to examine the behaviour of real exchange rates over relatively short time-periods has gained popularity among researchers, with Abuaf and Jorion (1990) and Hakkio (1984) representing early studies that use this approach in tests of PPP. Frankel and Rose (1996) apply panel-data regression tests to 45 years of annual data across 140 countries, to demonstrate a more accurate estimation of mean reversion in the real exchange rate. They argue that the use of panel data mitigates against the problems caused by structural shifts in exchange rate regimes, which are inherent in long time-series data. Additionally, since the bias in ordinary-least-squares estimates decreases as data variation increases, the size of PPP deviations would become sufficiently small relative to the total variation in the cross-sectional data, given that cross-sectional variation appears higher than time-series variation.[11]

However, while the use of the panel-data method is appealing in getting around the problems surrounding long-term time-series data, several criticisms have been levelled at the findings. Rogoff (1996) argues that findings of mean reversion tend to be much stronger when high-inflation countries are included in the sample, thus exaggerating the extent of convergence to PPP. Meanwhile, O'Connell (1996) points out that the standard practice of calculating real exchange rates relative to the US dollar could lead to cross-sectional dependence in time-series panel data, making it difficult to reject the null hypothesis of a random walk.

Empirical evidence in the 1990s

The majority of studies during the 1990s period focused on the bilateral exchange rates of industrialized countries with the US dollar;

although some have also tested the cross-rates against currencies other than the US dollar. The sample period most commonly investigated is the post-float era which began in 1973. Several studies have also incorporated the Bretton Woods fixed exchange rate regime, while a few have spanned various exchange rate regimes over a century or more in an attempt fully to capture the long-run effects of PPP. The choice of price series has also differed across studies, with the consumer price index (CPI) and wholesale price index (WPI) the most widely used. Occasionally, the gross domestic product (GDP) and gross national product (GNP) deflators have also been applied. The use of panel data has also become widespread during this time. Increasingly, studies in the second half of the 1990s have considered the PPP condition for developing countries.

Table 2.1 provides a comprehensive – but by no means exhaustive – summary of PPP research during the 1990s. Clearly, unit root and cointegration techniques have dominated the literature, even though a variety of approaches to testing for PPP has also been used. Indeed, the advancement of econometric time-series techniques such as these has been credited with boosting interest in the PPP doctrine. The Engle–Granger two-step test is the original test for cointegration.[12] The test applies either the standard or the augmented Dickey–Fuller test to the residual from the first-stage cointegrating regression of the exchange rate and price levels, to test for a unit root; an alternative test for cointegration may be done using an error correction model.[13]

On balance, research over the past decade appears to have been highly successful in proving that the PPP condition holds, across both industrialized and developing countries. Among the evidence in favour of long-run PPP in industrialized countries are those reported in Anker (1999), Bayoumi and MacDonald (1999), Flores et al. (1999), O'Connell (1998), Papell (1997), Papell and Theodoridis (1998), and Taylor and Sarno (1998). However, several papers using post-Bretton Woods time-series data reject the notion of PPP; for instance, Baum et al. (1999), Betton et al. (1995), Engel (2000) and Li (1999).

In contrast to the depth of empirical evidence available for the industrialized countries, research into the relationship between exchange rates and prices in developing countries has been relatively sparse. One obvious reason for this is the relatively limited data available for these emerging markets compared to the developed countries.

Table 2.1 Summary of PPP research in the 1990s

Author(s)	Nature of data	Sample countries	Sample period	Price index used	Approach	Does PPP hold?
A. Industrialized countries						
Abuaf and Jorion (1990)	Time-series and panel	10 countries, plus the US as reference country	1900–72 (A), 1973–87 (M)	CPI	OLS and SUR (GLS)	Yes
Anker (1999)	Panel	18 (14) countries	1974–97 (Q)	CPI (WPI)	Panel unit-root test (GLS)	Yes
Bahmani-Oskooee (1992)	Time-series	G-7 countries	1960–88 (A)	GNP deflator	Unit-root and cointegration tests	No
Baum et al. (1999)	Time-series	17 and 12 countries	1973–95 (M)	CPI, WPI	Fractional cointegration and structural break tests	No
Bayoumi and MacDonald (1999)	Panel	20 countries, 48 states (US), 9 provinces (Canada)	1973–93, 1972–94, 1963–92 (A)	CPI, WPI	Panel unit-root test	Yes
Betton et al. (1995)	Time-series	10 countries	1973–93 (M)	CPI	Two-way linear regression	No
Diebold et al. (1991)	Time-series	6 countries	From 1790s (A)	CPI, WPI	Gaussian likelihood tests	Yes
Edison and Fisher (1991)	Time-series	6 European countries	1973–88 (M)	CPI	Unit-root and cointegration test	Mixed, depends on exchange rate regime
Edison et al. (1997)	Time-series	13 countries	1974–92 (Q)	CPI	Cointegration test	Yes

Study	Type	Countries	Period	Price index	Method	PPP holds?
Engel (2000)	Time-series	UK and the US	1970–95 (Q)	GDP deflator	Unit-root and cointegration tests	No
Engel and Kim (1999)	Time-series	UK and the US	1985–95 (M)	PPI	Markov switching and cointegration tests	Inconclusive
Engel and Rogers (1996)	Panel	14 US cities; 9 Canadian cities	1978–97 (M; bi-M)	CPI for 14 goods	OLS with location and distance effects	No
Engel et al. (1997)	Panel	4 pairs of cities in the US and Europe	1978–94 (M)	CPI	GLS applied to a system of error-correction models	No
Fisher and Park (1991)	Time-series	G-10 countries	1973–88 (M)	CPI, WPI	Cointegration and unit-root tests	Yes
Flores et al. (1999)	Panel	10 countries	1973–94 (M)	CPI	Panel unit-root test (SUR-GLS)	Yes
Fung and Lo (1992)	Time-series	6 countries, plus the US as reference country	1979–89 (M)	CPI	Univariate and multivariate unit-root tests	Yes
Ghosh and Wolf (1994)	Panel and time-series	10 countries, plus the UK as reference country	1973–90	CPI, cover prices of The Economist magazine	Regression analysis and cointegration tests	No
Grilli and Kaminski (1991)	Time-series	UK and the US	1885–1986 (M)	CPI, WPI	Unit-root and variance ratio tests	Mixed, depends on historical period
Johnson (1993)	Time-series	Canada and the US	1870–1991 (M, A)	GNP deflator, CPI, WPI	Cointegration and unit-root tests	Yes
Koedijk et al. (1998)	Panel	17 countries	1972–96 (Q)	CPI	A numeraire-invariant panel method	Yes
Kuo and Mikkola (1999)	Time-series	UK and the US	1859–1992 (A)	WPI, GNP deflator	Stationarity test	Yes

Table 2.1 Continued

Author(s)	Nature of data	Sample countries	Sample period	Price index used	Approach	Does PPP hold?
Li (1999)	Time-series	29, 26 and 25 countries	1974–96 (A)	CPI	Hierarchical model	No
Lothian and Taylor (1996)	Time-series	France and the US, plus UK as reference country	1791–1990 (A)	WPI	Unit-root test	Yes
Maeso-Fernández (1998)	Time-series	19 countries	1974–92 (M, A)	CPI, WPI	Variance ratio tests	Yes
Manzur (1990)	Time-series	G7 countries, with the US as reference country	1973–86(Q)	CPI	Divisia index numbers	Yes
Michael et al. (1997)	Time-series	France, Germany, UK and the US	1921–25 (M); 1800–1992 (A)	WPI	Non-linear adjustment (STAR model)	Yes
O'Connell (1998)	Panel	64 countries	1973–95 (Q)	CPI	Panel unit-root test (GLS)	No
Papell (1997)	Panel	17 and 20 countries	1973–94 (M, Q)	CPI	Panel unit-root tests (FGLS incorporating serial correlation)	Yes
Papell and Theodoridis (1998)	Panel	20 countries	1973–96 (Q)	CPI	Panel unit-root test (GLS)	Yes
Parkes and Savvides (1999)	Panel	G-7 countries	1917–94 (A)	CPI, WPI	SUR and sequential tests for structural breaks	Yes
Patel (1990)	Time-series	6 countries	1974–86 (Q)	WPI	Cointegration and unit-root tests	No
Rogers (1995)	Time-series	UK and the US	1859–1992 (A)	WPI, GNP deflator	Cointegration and unit-root tests	Yes

Study	Method	Data	Period	Price index	Technique	Cointegration
Rogers and Jenkins (1995)	Time-series	11 countries; 54 different commodities from Canada and the US; 22 goods and services in 6 US and Canadian cities	1973–91 (M)	CPI components	Cointegration and unit-root tests	No
Sjaastad (1998)	Time-series	Switzerland and the US	1974–91 (Q)	GDP deflator, CPI, PPI	Commodity currency model	Yes
Taylor and Sarno (1998)	Panel	France, Germany, Japan, UK and the US	1973–96 (Q)	CPI, GDP deflator	Unit-root test (SUR-GLS)	Yes
Wei and Parsley (1995)	Panel	12 tradable sectors in 14 countries	1973–86 (A)	Sector-specific price deflators	OLS incorporating exchange rate volatility, transportation costs and cultural effects	Yes

B. Industrialized and developing countries

Study	Method	Data	Period	Price index	Technique	Cointegration
Cheung and Lai (2000)	Time-series	94 countries	1973–1994 (M)	CPI	Fractional integration model	Yes
Frankel and Rose (1996)	Panel	150 countries, plus the US as reference country	1948–92 (A)	CPI	OLS with time- and country-specific effects	Yes
Higgins and Zakrajsek (1999)	Panel	11 European countries, 12 OECD countries and 17 open economies	1973 (or 76 or 79)–97 (Q)	CPI, WPI	Four panel unit-root tests	Yes
Lee (1999)	Time-series	13 Asia Pacific countries	1957–94 (Q)	CPI, WPI	Generalized error-correction model	Yes

Table 2.1 Continued

Author(s)	Nature of data	Sample countries	Sample period	Price index used	Approach	Does PPP hold?
Phylaktis and Kassimatis (1994)	Panel	8 Pacific Basin countries, plus the US as reference country	1974–87 (M)	CPI, WPI	Cointegration and panel unit-root tests (GLS)	Yes
Wu and Chen (1999)	Panel	8 Pacific Basin countries, plus the US as reference country	1980–96 (M)	CPI, WPI	Two panel unit-root tests	No
C. Developing countries						
Bahmani-Oskooee (1998)	Time-series	11 Middle-Eastern countries	1971–94 (Q)	CPI	Stationarity test	Yes
Boyd and Smith (1999)	Panel	31 developing countries	1966–90 (Q)	CPI	Cointegration and panel unit-root tests	Yes
Doganlar (1999)	Time-series	India, Indonesia, Pakistan, Turkey and the Philippines	1980–95 (Q)	CPI	Cointegration tests	No
Guimaraes-Filho (1999)	Time-series	Brazil	1855–1990 (Q)	Unknown	Robust rank tests	No
Luintel (2000)	Panel	8 Asian developing countries	1958–89 (M)	CPI	Panel unit-root and variance ratio tests	Yes
Nagayasu (1998)	Panel	16 African countries	1981–94 (A)	CPI, WPI	Cointegration test	Yes
Salehizadeh and Taylor (1999)	Time-series	27 American, European, African and Asian emerging economies	1975–97 (M)	CPI	Cointegration test	Yes
Sarno (2000)	Time-series	11 Middle-Eastern countries	1973–94 (Q)	CPI	Multivariate non-linear models	Yes

The empirical evidence – largely based on the cointegration approach – for countries in the Middle-East, East Asia, Latin America, Africa and Eastern Europe suggests that PPP generally holds in these markets (Bahmani-Oskooee, 1998; Boyd and Smith, 1999; Luintel, 2000; Nagayasu, 1998; Salehizadeh and Taylor, 1999; Sarno, 2000). Research combining both developing and developed countries, such as Cheung and Lai (2000), Frankel and Rose (1996) and Lee (1999), have provided supporting evidence for PPP. Phylaktis and Kassimatis (1994) find evidence of PPP for eight Pacific Basin countries (including Japan); interestingly, they find that deviations from PPP take only about a year to be reduced by half, in contrast to the findings for other industrial countries as discussed in the previous section. In contrast, Wu and Chen (1999), also using panel unit-root tests, disprove the existence of PPP for the same countries tested by Phylaktis and Kassimatis, albeit over a different time-period.

To date, the empirical findings for developing countries have been based on data up to the start of the Asian financial crisis in 1997. The 'de-pegging' of exchange rates in East Asia following the onset of the Asian financial crisis in 1997, as well as in some Latin American countries in recent times, should provide fertile opportunities for further research into the PPP condition in emerging markets. Indeed, Phylaktis and Kassimatis tried to capture implications of floating exchange rates for the Asian countries in their sample by using the 'black market' rates rather than the 'managed' official exchange rates. Tests of exchange rate behaviour under the pre- versus post-crisis regime – as these countries increasingly liberalize their financial markets and more and better-quality data become available – would be an interesting area of study similar to that comparing the pre- and post-Bretton Woods periods for the industrialized countries.

The Economist's Big Mac Index

The introduction of the Big Mac Index (BMI) by *The Economist* magazine in 1986 – in the manner of a tongue-in-cheek approach to PPP – has undoubtedly sharpened interest in the doctrine of the 'law of one price'. The BMI essentially provides a 'quick and nasty' method of valuing exchange rates. The relative prices of homogeneous Big Mac hamburgers in two countries are compared against the rate of exchange between their two currencies; the currency of one country is said to be either over- or under-valued relative to the other, in the event that the price relative and the exchange rate are not equal.

Economic research on this Index has evolved into an important strand of PPP literature known as 'burgernomics', a term coined by *The Economist*. Interestingly, financial markets appear to have become increasingly taken with the idea of using the Index as a practical approach to valuing currencies and in making international price comparisons.

In the burgernomics literature, Cumby (1996) first used the BMI to test rigorously for the PPP condition, with the conclusion that deviations from Big Mac PPP are actually useful for forecasting exchange rates. Pakko and Pollard (1996) and Click (1996) examine the nature of deviations from Big Mac PPP, while Annaert and Ceuster (1997) investigate the value of BMI from an investment perspective. Ong (1997) improves upon the BMI and proposes the 'No-Frills Index' to value currencies, wherein the concept of productivity bias is taken into account in deriving an enhanced index. Recently, Lan (2001) derived the long-run equilibrium values of currencies from the Big Mac data, by using Monte Carlo methods to analyse the entire distribution of the estimated equilibrium exchange rates and estimate the adjustment paths of actual rates into the future. Other applications of the BMI include Ong (1998a), where the BMI is shown to have accurately predicted the Asian currency crisis of 1997/98, and Ong (1998b) and Ong and Mitchell (2000), who use the BMI to compare the purchasing power of earnings and cost-of-living around the world. These topics are covered in the following chapters of this book.

To measure the extent of both commercial and academic interest in the BMI, a search for the exact phrase 'Big Mac Index' was performed on the web search engine, Google.[14] This resulted in 697 'hits'.[15] These BMI web sites were subsequently categorized according to language and institutional domain, as presented in Table 2.2. The left panel of the Table 2.2 records the search results by language, with 17 languages identified and the remaining 30 per cent of sites not specifically identified by language. English websites number the most, followed by European languages. Developing countries in both Europe and Asia also have sites dedicated to this widely-followed innovation of *The Economist*.

Table 2.2 Big Mac Index search results

Language of web page	Number	Institutional domain	Number
English	405	.com	271
Danish, French, German, Japanese, Swedish	66	.edu	131
Chinese, Dutch, Italian, Korea, Norwegian, Russian, Spanish	27	.org	45
Czech, Finnish, Hungarian, Portuguese	7	.net	38
Other	192	Other	260
Total	697	Total	745

Source: Lan (2002).

The right panel of Table 2.2 suggests that the BMI is used across many sectors. Only 20 per cent of BMI pages are related to educational activities (as represented by the '.edu' domain), with the majority of webpages dedicated to the BMI created by non-educational parties. This points to the practical versatility of the Index, presumably because of the simple and timely nature of the metric.

Summary

Interest in the purchasing power parity concept has continued to grow unabated, 80 years after its resurrection by Gustav Cassel. Indeed, if anything, work in the area has grown at a relatively quicker rate since the 1970s than in most other major topics in economics. This is despite the momentary hiccup in confidence following the collapse of the Bretton Woods system and the move to the floating rate regime. Over time, there have been clear trends in the research methods used, as well as the corresponding findings on the validity of the PPP condition. Prior to the mid-1980s, empirical tests using OLS and GLS methods tended to reject the PPP condition. The advancement of econometric models in the latter part of the 1980s, notably the introduction of unit root and cointegration techniques, has provided better support for the theory of PPP. In particular, the use of longer time-horizon data and cross-sectional, or panel, data are seen to have improved the 'power' of those tests, and thus provide more reliable results and increased confidence in the theory of PPP. Another source of inspiration for PPP research in recent years has been the use of *The Economist*'s Big Mac Index, which has spawned a strand of research – aptly coined 'burgernomics' – since its introduction in 1986. Empirical tests using the BMI to explain exchange rate movements have been surprisingly successful in exploring the PPP condition, and are increasingly accepted as a practical approach to valuing currencies.

Notes

1. Friedman and Schwartz (1963) and Gaillot (1970) find evidence to support PPP over long periods of time.
2. See Frenkel (1981).
3. A detailed exposition on Dornbusch's 'overshooting' model is provided by Rogoff (2002).
4. Figure 2.1 plots, on the left-hand axis, the number of articles in each decade for the six topics. As the left vertical axis uses a logarithmic scale, the change in the height of the bars from one decade to the next indicates an exponential rate of growth for each topic. The right vertical axis gives the average rate of growth on an annual basis for each topic.
5. See Frenkel (1981).
6. For instance, Manzur (1990) uses the Divisia index number method to show that while short-run variability in exchange rates does not reflect the inflation differentials during the corresponding period, PPP actually holds quite well in the long run, which in that instance is identified as five years.
7. Edison *et al.* (1997) demonstrate that the failure of PPP under the post-float regime is largely due to the low power of the tests employed, as a result of the small sample size. They argue that the procedure pioneered by Horvath and Watson (1995), which makes use of the same vector autoregression as the Johansen (1991) procedure, but with restriction, has greater testing power.
8. See MacDonald and Stein (1999) for a discussion on extending the span of the data sample.
9. Rogers (1995) presents evidence that wars have a significant effect in moving nominal exchange rates and relative price levels away from the long-run path implied by PPP.
10. Mussa (1986) shows that real exchange rates tend to be more volatile under the floating rate regime compared to fixed exchange rates.
11. See Davutyan and Pippenger (1985).
12. Engle and Granger (1987) define a set of non-stationary series, integrated of the same order, to be cointegrated when some linear combination of these series produces a series that is stationary. In other words, if a set of non-stationary series share common trends so that the trends cancel each other out when linearly combined, they are said to be cointegrated.

13. Breuer (1994) provides a comprehensive overview on the different aspects and tests of PPP studies – including the different forms of cointegration and unit-root tests – over time, covering research up to the early 1990s.
14. The address of the Google search engine is http://www.google.com
15. According to Lan (2002), the search results are compiled as follows: (1) to narrow down the search, an additional constraint 'not computer' is used; (2) all the search results in Google refer to the returned entries excluding pages similar to those displayed; and (3) another 18 entries from Google contain only the word 'Burgernomics', but not the phrase 'Big Mac Index'.

References

Abuaf, N. and P. Jorion (1990) 'Purchasing Power Parity in the Long Run', *Journal of Finance*, vol. 45, pp. 157–74.

Adler, M. and B. Lehmann (1983) 'Deviations from Purchasing Power Parity in the Long Run', *Journal of Finance*, vol. 38, pp. 1471–87.

Anker, P. (1999) 'Pitfalls in Panel Tests of Purchasing Power Parity', *Weltwischaftliches Archiv*, vol. 135, pp. 437–53.

Annaert, J. and M. J. K. Ceuster (1997) 'The Big Mac: More Than a Junk Asset Allocator?' *International Review of Financial Analysis*, vol. 6, pp. 179–92.

Bahmani-Oskooee, M. (1992) 'A Time-Series Approach to Test the Productivity Bias Hypothesis in Purchasing Power Parity', *Kyklos*, vol. 45, pp. 227–36.

Bahmani-Oskooee, M. (1998) 'Do Exchange Rates Follow a Random Walk Process in Middle Eastern Countries?', *Economics Letters*, vol. 58, pp. 339–44.

Baum, C. F., J. T. Barkoulas and M. Caglayan (1999) 'Long Memory or Structural Breaks: Can Either Explain Non-stationary Real Exchange Rates under the Current Float?', *Journal of International Financial Markets, Institutions and Money*, vol. 9, pp. 359–76.

Bayoumi, T. and R. MacDonald (1999) 'Deviations of Exchange Rates from Purchasing Power Parity: A Story Featuring Two Monetary Unions', *IMF Staff Papers*, no. 46, pp. 89–102.

Betton, S., M. D. Levi and R. Uppal (1995) 'Index-Induced Errors and Purchasing Power Parity: Bounding the Possible Bias', *Journal of International Financial Markets, Institutions and Money*, vol. 5, pp. 165–79.

Boyd, D. and R. Smith (1999) 'Testing for Purchasing Power Parity: Econometric Issues and an Application to Developing Countries', *The Manchester School of Economic and Social Studies*, vol. 67, pp. 287–303.

Breuer, J. B. (1994) 'An Assessment of the Evidence on Purchasing Power Parity', in *Estimating Equilibrium Exchange Rates*, ed. J. Williamson, pp. 245–77. Washington, DC: Institute for International Economics.

Cheung, Y. W. and K. S. Lai (2000) 'On Cross-Country Differences in the Persistence of Real Exchange Rates', *Journal of International Economics*, vol. 50, pp. 375–97.

Click, R. W. (1996) 'Contrarian MacParity', *Economics Letters*, vol. 53, pp. 209–12.

Corbae, D. and S. Ouliaris (1988) 'Cointegration and Tests of Purchasing Power Parity', *Review of Economics and Statistics*, vol. 70, pp. 508–21.

Cumby, R. E. (1996) 'Forecasting Exchange Rates and Relative Prices with the Hamburger Standard: Is What You Want What You Get with McParity?', NBER Working Paper Series, no. 5675, National Bureau of Economic Research, Cambridge, Massachusetts.

Davutyan, N. and J. Pippenger (1985) 'Purchasing Power Parity did not Collapse during the 1970s', *American Economic Review*, vol. 75, pp. 1151–8.

Dickey, D. A. and W. A. Fuller (1979) 'Distribution of the Estimators for Autoregressive Time Series with a Unit Root', *Journal of the American Statistical Association*, vol. 74, pp. 427–31.

Diebold, F., S. Husted, and M. Rush (1991) 'Real Exchange Rate under the Gold Standard', *Journal of Political Economy*, vol. 99, pp. 1151–8.

Doganlar, M. (1999) 'Testing Long-Run Validity of Purchasing Power Parity for Asian Countries', *Applied Economics Letters*, vol. 6, pp. 147–51.

Dornbusch, R. (1976) 'Expectations and Exchange Rate Dynamics', *Journal of Political Economy*, vol. 84, pp. 1161–76.

Edison, H. J. and E. Fisher (1991) 'A Long-Run View of the European Monetary System', *Journal of International Money and Finance*, vol. 10, pp. 53–70.

Edison, H. J., G. E. Gagnon and W. R. Melick (1997) 'Understanding the Empirical Literature on Purchasing Power Parity: The Post-Bretton Woods Era', *Journal of International Money and Finance*, vol. 16, pp. 1–17.

Enders, W. (1988) 'ARIMA and Cointegration Tests of PPP under Fixed and Flexible Exchange Rate Regimes', *Review of Economics and Statistics*, vol. 70, pp. 504–8.

Engel, C. (2000) 'Long-Run PPP May Not Hold after All', *Journal of International Economics*, vol. 51, pp. 243–73.

Engel, C., M. K. Hendrickson and J. H. Rogers (1997) 'Intra-National, Intra-Continental and Intra-Planetary PPP', International Finance Discussion Papers' no. 589, Board of Governors of the Federal Reserve System, Washington DC.

Engel, C. and C. J. Kim (1999) 'The Long-Run US/UK Real Exchange Rate', *Journal of Money, Credit and Banking*, vol. 31, pp. 335–56.

Engel, C. and J. H. Rogers (1996) 'How Wide is the Border?', *American Economic Review*, vol. 86, pp. 1112–25.

Engle, R. F. and C. W. J. Granger (1987) 'Cointegration and Error Correction: Representation, Estimation, and Testing', *Econometrica*, vol. 55, pp. 251–76.

Fisher, E. and J. Park (1991) 'Testing Purchasing Power Parity under the Null Hypothesis of Co-Integration', *Economic Journal*, vol. 52, pp. 1476–84.

Flood, R. P. (1981) 'Explanation of Exchange Rate Volatility and Other Empirical Regularities in Some Popular Models of Foreign Exchange Market,' *Carnegie–Rochester Conference Series on Public Policy*, vol. 15, pp. 219–50.

Flores, R., P. Jorion, P. Preumont and A. Szafarz (1999) 'Multivariate Unit Root Tests of the PPP Hypothesis', *Journal of Empirical Finance*, vol. 6, pp. 335–53.

Frankel, J. A. (1986) 'International Capital Mobility and Crowding Out in the U.S. Economy: Imperfect Integration of Financial Markets or Goods

Markets?', in *How Open is the US Economy*, ed. R. Hafer, pp. 33–67. Massachusetts: Lexington Books.

Frankel, J. A. (1990) 'Zen and the Art of Modern Macroeconomics: A Commentary', in *Monetary Policy for a Volatile Global Economy*, eds W. S. Haraf and T. D. Willett, pp. 117–23. Washington, DC: American Enterprise Institute for Public Policy Research.

Frankel, J. A. and A. Rose (1996) 'A Panel Project on Purchasing Power Parity: Mean Reversion within and between Countries', *Journal of International Economics*, vol. 40, pp. 209–24.

Frenkel, J. A. (1981) 'The Collapse of Purchasing Power Parities during the 1970s', *European Economic Review*, vol. 16, pp. 145–65.

Friedman, M. and A. J. Schwartz (1963) *A Monetary History of the United States: 1867–1960*. Princeton: Princeton University Press.

Froot, K. A. and K. Rogoff (1995) 'Perspectives on PPP and Long-Run Real Exchange Rates', in *Handbook of International Economics*, eds G. Grossman and K. Rogoff, vol. 3, pp. 1647–88. Amsterdam: North-Holland Press.

Fung, H. G. and W. C. Lo (1992) 'Deviations from Purchasing Power Parity', *The Financial Review*, vol. 27, pp. 553–70.

Gaillot, H. J. (1970) 'Purchasing Power Parity as an Explanation of Long Term Changes in Exchange Rates', *Journal of Money, Credit and Banking*, vol. 2, pp. 348–57.

Ghosh, A. R. and Wolf, H. C. (1994) 'Pricing in International Markets: Lessons from *The Economist*', NBER Working Paper Series, no. 4806, National Bureau of Economic Research, Cambridge, Massachusetts.

Glen, J. D. (1992) 'Real Exchange Rates in the Short, Medium and Long Run', *Journal of International Economics*, vol. 33, pp. 147–66.

Grilli, V. and G. Kaminsky (1991) 'Nominal Exchange Rate Regimes and the Real Exchange Rate: Evidence for the United States and Great Britain, 1885–86', *Journal of Monetary Economics*, vol. 27, pp. 191–212.

Guimaraes-Filho, R. F. (1999) 'Does Purchasing Power Parity Hold after All? Evidence from a Robust Test', *Applied Financial Economics*, vol. 9, pp. 167–72.

Hakkio, C. (1984) 'A Reexamination of Purchasing Power Parity', *Journal of International Economics*, vol. 17, pp. 265–77.

Higgins, M. and E. Zakrajsek (1999) 'Purchasing Power Parity: Three Stakes through the Heart of the Unit Root Null', Staff Reports no. 80, Federal Reserve Bank of New York, New York.

Horvath, M. T. K. and M. W. Watson (1995) 'Testing for Cointegration when Some of the Cointegrating Vectors are Prespecified', *Econometric Theory*, vol. 11, pp. 952–84.

Johansen, S. (1991) 'Estimation and Hypothesis Testing of Cointegration Vectors in Gaussian Vector Autoregressive Models', *Econometrica*, vol. 59, pp. 1551–80.

Johnson, D. R. (1993) 'Unit Roots, Cointegration and Purchasing Power Parity: Canada and the United States, 1870–1991', in *The Exchange Rate and the Economy: Proceedings of a Conference Held at the Bank of Canada 22–23 June 1992*, pp. 133–98. Ottawa: Bank of Canada.

Koedijk, K. G., P. C. Schotman and M. A. Van Dijk (1998) 'The Re-Emergence of PPP in the 1990s', *Journal of International Money and Finance*, vol. 17, pp. 51–61.

Kuo, B. and A. Mikkola (1999) 'Re-Examining Long-Run Purchasing Power Parity', *Journal of International Money and Finance*, vol. 18, pp. 251–66.

Lan, Y. (2001) 'The Long-Run Value of Currencies: A Big Mac Perspective', paper presented to the 30th Annual Conference of Economists, the Economic Society of Australia, Perth.

Lan, Y. (2002) 'The Explosion of Purchasing Power Parity', in *Exchange Rates, Interest Rates and Commodity Prices*, ed. M. Manzur, pp. 9–39. Cheltenham, UK, and Northampton, USA: Edward Elgar Publishing.

Lee, D. Y. (1999) 'Purchasing Power Parity and Dynamic Error Correction: Evidence from Asia Pacific Economies', *International Review of Economics and Finance*, vol. 8, pp. 199–212.

Li, K. (1999) 'Testing Symmetry and Proportionality in PPP: A Panel-Data Approach', *Journal of Business and Economic Statistics*, vol. 17, pp. 409–18.

Lothian, J. R. and M. P. Taylor (1996) 'Real Exchange Rate Behavior: The Recent Float from the Perspective of the Past Two Centuries', *Journal of Political Economy*, vol. 104, pp. 488–510.

Luintel, K. B. (2000) 'Real Exchange Rate Behavior: Evidence from Black Markets', *Journal of Applied Econometrics*, vol. 15, pp. 161–85.

MacDonald, R. and J. L. Stein (1999) 'Introduction: Equilibrium Exchange Rates', in *Equilibrium Exchange Rates*, eds R. MacDonald and J. L. Stein, pp. 1–17. Boston/Dordrecht/London: Kluwer Academic Publishers.

Maeso-Fernández, F. (1998) 'Econometric Methods and Purchasing Power Parity: Short- and Long-Run PPP', *Applied Economics*, vol. 30, pp. 1443–57.

Manzur, M. (1990) 'An International Comparison of Prices and Exchange Rates: A New Test of Purchasing Power Parity', *Journal of International Money and Finance*, vol. 9, pp. 75–91.

Manzur, M. (1993) *Exchange Rates, Prices and World Trade: New Methods, Evidence and Implications*. London: Routledge.

Mark, N. (1990) 'Real Exchange Rates in the Long Run: An Empirical Investigation', *Journal of International Economics*, vol. 28, pp. 115–36.

Meese, R. and K. Rogoff (1988) 'Was it Real? The Exchange Rate Interest Differential Relation over the Modern Floating Exchange Rate Period', *Journal of Finance*, vol. 43, pp. 933–48.

Michael, P., A. Nobay and D. Peel (1997) 'Transaction Costs and Non-Linear Adjustments in Real Exchange Rates: An Empirical Investigation', *Journal of Political Economy*, vol. 105, pp. 862–79.

Mussa, M. (1982) 'A Model of Exchange Rate Dynamics,' *Journal of Political Economy*, vol. 90, pp. 74–104.

Mussa, M. (1986) 'Nominal Exchange Rate Regimes and the Behavior of Real Exchange Rates: Evidence and Implications', *Carnegie-Rochester Conference Series on Public Policy*, vol. 25, pp. 117–213.

Nagayasu, J. (1998) 'Does the Long-Run PPP Hypothesis Hold for Africa? Evidence from Panel Co-Integration Study', IMF Working Paper no. 98/123, International Monetary Fund, Washington, DC.

O'Connell, P. G. J. (1998) 'The Overvaluation of Purchasing Power Parity', *Journal of International Economics*, vol. 44, pp. 1–19.

Ong, L. L. (1997) 'Burgernomics: The Economics of the Big Mac Standard', *Journal of International Money and Finance*, vol. 16, pp. 865–78.

Ong, L. L. (1998a) 'Burgernomics and the ASEAN Currency Crisis', *Journal of the Australian Society of Security Analysts*, Autumn, pp. 15–16.

Ong, L. L. (1998b) 'Big Mac and Wages to Go, Please: Comparing the Purchasing Power of Earnings around the World', *Australian Journal of Labor Economics*, vol. 2, pp. 53–68.

Ong, L. L. and J. D. Mitchell (2000) 'Professors and Hamburgers: An International Comparison of Real Academic Salaries', *Applied Economics*, vol. 32, pp. 869–76.

Pakko, M. R. and P. S. Pollard (1996) 'For Here to Go? Purchasing Power Parity and the Big Mac', *Federal Reserve Bank of St. Louis Review*, vol. 78, pp. 3–21.

Papell, D. H. (1997) 'Searching for Stationarity: Purchasing Power Parity under the Current Float', *Journal of International Economics*, vol. 43, pp. 313–32.

Papell, D. H. and H. Theodoridis (1998) 'Increasing Evidence of Purchasing Power Parity over the Current Float', *Journal of International Money and Finance*, vol. 17, pp. 41–50.

Parkes, A. L. H. and A. Savvides (1999) 'Purchasing Power Parity in the Long Run and Structural Breaks: Evidence from Real Sterling Exchange Rates', *Applied Financial Economics*, vol. 9, pp. 117–27.

Patel, J. (1990) 'Purchasing Power Parity as a Long-Run Relation', *Journal of Applied Econometrics*, vol. 5, pp. 367–79.

Phylaktis, K. and Y. Kassimatis (1994) 'Does the Real Exchange Rate Follow a Random Walk? The Pacific Basin Perspective', *Journal of International Money and Finance*, vol. 13, pp. 476–95.

Rogers, J. H. (1995) 'Real Shocks and Real Exchange Rates in Really Long-Term Data', International Finance Discussion Papers, no. 493, Board of Governors of the Federal Reserve System, Washington, DC.

Rogers, J. H. and M. Jenkins (1995) 'Haircuts or Hysteresis? Sources of Movements in Real Exchange Rates', *Journal of International Economics*, vol. 38, pp. 339–60.

Rogoff, K. (1996) 'The Purchasing Power Parity Puzzle', *Journal of Economic Literature*, vol. 34, pp. 647–68.

Rogoff, K. (2002) 'Dornbusch's Overshooting Model after Twenty-Five Years', IMF Working Paper no. 02/39, International Monetary Fund, Washington, DC.

Salehizadeh, M. and R. Taylor (1999) 'A Test of Purchasing Power Parity for Emerging Economies', *Journal of International Financial Markets, Institutions and Money*, vol. 9, pp. 183–93.

Sarno, L. (2000) 'Real Exchange Rate Behaviour in the Middle East: A Re-examination', *Economics Letters*, vol. 66, pp. 127–36.

Sjaastad, L. (1998) 'On Exchange Rates, Nominal and Real', *Journal of International Money and Finance*, vol. 17, pp. 407–39.

Taylor, M. P. and L. Sarno (1998) 'The Behavior of Real Exchange Rates during the Post-Bretton Woods Period', *Journal of International Economics*, vol. 46, pp. 281–312.

Wei, S. and D. Parsley (1995) 'Purchasing Power Disparity during the Floating Rate Period: Exchange Rate Volatility and Trade Barriers', NBER Working Paper Series, no. 5032, National Bureau of Economic Research, Cambridge, Massachusetts.

Wu, J. L. and S. L. Chen (1999) 'Are Real Exchange Rates Stationary Based on Panel Unit-Root Tests? Evidence from Pacific Basin Countries', *International Journal of Finance and Economics*, vol. 4, pp. 243–52.

3
The Economics of the Big Mac Standard*

Suppose a man climbs five feet up a sea wall, then climbs down 12 feet. Whether he drowns or not depends upon how high above sea-level he was when he started. The same problem arises in deciding whether currencies are under- or over-valued.

(*The Economist*, 29 August 1995, p. 70)

In the course of purchasing power parity (PPP) research, much of the debate over validity has been over the choice of an *appropriate* 'basket' for making purchasing power comparisons. The different compositions of goods and services in these baskets across countries have resulted in arguments against their usefulness for PPP purposes. This problem is augmented by the existence of productivity differentials in traded and non-traded goods across countries. Therefore, we consider the use of the Big Mac hamburger as the international monetary standard as being a more palatable alternative. It is produced locally in over 80 countries around the world, with only minor changes in recipe, and thus has the flavour of the 'perfect universal commodity'. Our results indicate that the Big Mac Index is surprisingly accurate in tracking exchange rates over the long-term, which is consistent with previous PPP research findings. We subsequently enhance our PPP comparisons by taking into account the productivity differentials between countries and excluding non-traded goods from the Big Mac Index to derive the No-Frills Index.

---

* A revised version of this chapter was published in the *Journal of International Money and Finance*, vol. 16, pp. 865–78 (1997).

Introduction

The theory of PPP states that the rate of exchange between two currencies is determined by the price levels in the two economies. In other words, the prices of a basket of similar goods and services in two countries *should be equal* when converted to a common currency. To the extent that the prices are *not* equalized, the exchange rate is said to be misaligned. As discussed in Chapter 1, there has been much debate over the choice of an appropriate 'basket' for making PPP comparisons in the course of PPP research over the years.[1] Clearly, the different compositions of goods and services across the different indices commonly used in tests of PPP – and the extent to which these items affect the exchange rates – have resulted in arguments over their usefulness.[2]

Given the prevailing index-number problem, we have decided to use the Big Mac as the international monetary standard in this test of PPP, in place of the traditional basket of goods and services. Our decision is based on the fact that the Big Mac is considered the 'perfect universal commodity': it is produced locally in more than 80 countries around the world, measures 95 mm in diameter, weighs 205 g, and generally uses the same ingredients everywhere – two beef patties, a special sauce, lettuce, cheese, pickles and a sesame-seed bun.[3] As well as being a 'standard product', this means that its local prices are less likely to be distorted by international transportation and distribution costs.[4] Furthermore, since the Big Mac comprises both traded and non-traded goods, we are able to incorporate the productivity bias concept into our research. Thus, the main objectives of this chapter are to (1) analyze the productivity bias problem in greater detail using the Big Mac hamburger; and (2) improve on the Big Mac Index by introducing the No-Frills Index, which takes into account the productivity differentials between countries.

Our results indicate that the Big Mac Index performs just as well as, if not better than, most indices used in tests of PPP. Overall, we find that the Index is surprisingly accurate in tracking exchange rates over the long term (that is, the nine years of our sample period), which is also consistent with previous research findings.[5] Even though individual currencies may deviate from the Big Mac PPP on a country-by-country basis, there is a distinct tendency for deviations to offset one another so that the world currencies, in aggregate, are at parity for any one particular year. Moreover, geographic influences appear to play an important role in currency valuation. We show that PPP comparisons can be enhanced by taking into account the productivity differentials between countries and excluding non-traded goods from the Big Mac Index to derive the No-Frills Index.

This chapter is organized as follows. The next section details the data, followed by an examination of currency valuation relative to the Big Mac PPP. We then look at the role of geography in determining currency values, and carry out further tests of absolute parity using regression analysis, followed by tests of relative parity. We subsequently present a discussion on possible reasons for observed departures from PPP. Following on, we decompose the Big Mac into its traded and non-traded components in order to enhance PPP comparisons, and the chapter concludes with a summary of our findings.

The data

The data used in this study consist of the prices of McDonald's Big Mac hamburgers in 34 countries expressed in terms of the respective domestic currencies and the corresponding exchange rates. These are published annually in *The Economist* magazine over the 1986 to 1994 period; an example of the data available is shown in Figure 3.1.

Looking at the first two columns of the figure, the cost of a Big Mac in Australia is A$2.45 which is the equivalent of US$1.76. This US dollar equivalent is calculated by converting the Australian price at the actual exchange rate of A$1.39 = US$1.00, which is given in the third column. The US dollar cost of the Australian Big Mac of US$1.76 is to be compared with the cost of a Big Mac in the US of US$2.28, given as the first entries in columns 1 and 2 of Figure 3.1. Consequently, hamburgers are relatively cheaper in Australia.

The implied PPP of the Australian dollar is derived by dividing the domestic currency price of A$2.45 by the US Big Mac price of US$2.28, 2.45/2.28 = 1.07. This means that, on the basis of Big Mac prices, the exchange rate should be A$1.07 per US dollar, as shown in the fourth column of Figure 3.1. Given the actual rate of A$1.39 per US dollar (column 3), the Australian dollar is undervalued by 23 per cent, as indicated in column 5.

Big Mac prices		Actual exchange rate 13/4/93	Implied PPP† of the dollar	Local currency under(−) over(+) valuation **, %
Prices in local currency*	Prices in dollars			
United States‡	$2.28	2.28	−	−	−
Argentina	Peso3.60	3.60	1.00	1.58	+58
Australia	A$2.45	1.76	1.39	1.07	−23
Belgium	BFr109	3.36	32.45	47.81	+47
Brazil	Cr77000	2.80	27521	33772	+23
Britain	£1.79	2.79	1.56	33.772	+23
Canada	C$2.76	2.19	1.56‡‡	1.27‡‡	+23
China	Yuan8.50	1.50	5.68	3.73	−34
Denmark	DKr25.75	4.25	6.06	11.29	+86
France	FFr18.50	3.46	5.34	8.11	+52
Germany	DM4.60	2.91	1.58	2.02	+28
Holland	F15.45	3.07	1.77	3.39	+35
Hong Kong	HK$9.00	1.16	7.73	3.95	−49
Hungary	Forint157	1.78	88.18	68.86	−22
Ireland	I£1.48	2.29	1.54‡‡	1.54‡‡	0
Italy	Lire4500	2.95	1523	1974	+30
Japan	¥391	3.45	113	171	+51
Malaysia	Ringgit3.35	1.30	2.58	1.47	−43
Mexico	Peso7.09	2.29	3.10	3.11	0
Russia	Rouble780	1.14	686§	342	−50
S. Korea	Won2300	2.89	796	1009	+27
Spain	Ptas325	2.85	114	143	+25
Sweden	SKr25.50	3.43	7.43	11.18	+50
Switzerland	SwFr5.70	3.94	1.45	2.50	+72
Thailand	Baht48	1.91	25.16	21.05	−16

Figure 3.1 The hamburger standard

Note: McDonald's *Prices may vary locally; †Purchasing power parity: local price divided by price in United States; **Against dollar; ‡Average of New York, Chicago, San Francisco and Atlanta; ‡‡Dollars per pound; §Market rate.

Source: © The Economist Newspaper Limited, London, 17 April 1993, p.83. Reproduced with permission.

The valuation of currencies

In this section we investigate the valuation of currencies relative to their Big Mac PPP. Let P_{ct} be the domestic currency price of a Big Mac in country c in year t; P_t^* be the price in US dollars of a Big Mac in the US; and S_{ct} be the spot exchange rate, defined as the domestic currency cost of US$1. Accordingly, P_{ct}/P_t^* is the Big Mac PPP. Consider the ratio of this PPP to the actual exchange rate:

$$R_{ct} \equiv \frac{P_{ct}/P_t^*}{S_{ct}} \tag{3.1}$$

One way to determine whether or not the currency is over- or undervalued is to analyse the extent to which the ratio in equation (3.1) departs from unity: it is overvalued (undervalued) if it is greater (less) than 1, and at parity if it is equivalent to 1. However, it is more convenient to express the ratio in (3.1), in logarithmic form:

$$r_{ct} \equiv \log\left(\frac{P_{ct}/P_t^*}{S_{ct}}\right) = \log\frac{P_{ct}}{P_t^*} - \log S_{ct} \tag{3.2}$$

Thus, a currency is said to be overvalued if r_{ct} is greater than 0, undervalued if r_{ct} is less than 0, and at parity if r_{ct} equals 0. Note that $r_{ct} \times 100$ is approximately the percentage deviation from parity.

Table 3.1 gives r_{ct} for each country and year, as well as the row and column averages, r_c and $r_{\cdot t}$. Looking at column 10 of the table, Chile appears closest to achieving parity, with an average undervaluation of only 0.5 per cent. The Hong Kong dollar is undervalued against the US dollar by 68 per cent, while the Danish krone is overvalued by 57 per cent. The last row of Table 3.1 shows that these currencies are, on average, overvalued against the US dollar, with 1987 recording a high of 33 per cent. In other words, the US dollar is undervalued on average. The years 1988 and 1994 are the exceptions, with average undervaluations of 9 and 0.4 per cent respectively.

Figure 3.2 shows r_c, the country averages of the over-/undervaluations. We find that over the 1986 to 1994 period, 14 currencies are, on average, undervalued against the US dollar. The remaining currencies are above the grand average of 6.6 per cent.

Next, we test whether or not the deviations from parity are significant. Table 3.2 provides the results of t-tests in the form of the

Table 3.1 Domestic currency valuation relative to the US dollar ($r_{ct} \times 100$), 1986–94

Country	1986 (1)	1987 (2)	1988 (3)	1989 (4)	1990 (5)	1991 (6)	1992 (7)	1993 (8)	1994 (9)	Average (10)
1. Argentina	–	–	–	–	–	–	42.22	45.74	45.11	44.36
2. Australia	–40.85	–	–50.59	–17.59	–22.88	–15.28	–12.16	–26.16	–28.30	–26.73
3. Austria	–	–	–	–	–	–	–	–	20.97	20.97
4. Belgium	28.77	36.29	7.90	13.04	23.89	25.32	38.53	38.75	29.74	26.91
5. Brazil	–57.05	–	–	–	–	–	–21.59	20.47	–37.54	–23.93
6. Britain	2.94	4.32	–7.70	4.96	4.80	27.87	32.64	21.06	13.94	11.65
7. Canada	–16.38	–	–36.59	–11.57	–14.84	–10.05	5.72	24.05	–11.42	–12.40
8. Chile	–	–	–	–	–	–	–	–	–0.48	–0.48
9. China	–	–	–	–	–	–	–63.60	–42.05	–79.98	–61.88
10. Czech Republic	–	–	–	–	–	–	–	–	–31.38	–31.38
11. Denmark	–	62.55	40.34	51.76	59.63	61.63	67.72	62.22	51.53	57.17
12. France	43.75	54.64	25.15	31.86	35.76	34.78	39.76	41.79	32.14	37.74
13. Germany	27.52	30.34	3.55	11.95	14.90	13.43	22.31	24.57	15.67	18.25
14. Greece	–	–	–	–	–	–	–	–	7.30	7.30
15. Holland	17.65	27.71	8.75	16.81	24.00	21.46	28.22	30.03	21.58	21.80
16. Hong Kong	–49.60	–	–89.72	–72.71	–69.19	–67.66	–64.39	–67.14	–65.88	–68.29
17. Hungary	–	–	–	–	–	–38.51	–27.18	–24.73	–33.77	–31.05
18. Ireland	0.00	5.49	–19.53	–10.38	–6.56	0.00	7.88	0.00	18.68	–2.89
19. Italy	–	43.01	11.59	16.75	36.57	25.57	41.76	25.94	49.14	27.48
20. Japan	40.55	–	22.31	31.91	5.51	22.46	26.87	41.43	49.48	30.02
21. Malaysia	–	–	–	–	–	–	–	–	–49.48	–52.87
22. Mexico	–	–	–	–	–	–	–	–	4.65	7.82
23. Poland	–	–	–	–	–	–	–	–	–50.95	–50.95
24. Portugal	–	–	–	–	–	–	–	–	9.32	9.32

25. Russia	-20.59	-	-	-	104.15	93.68	-131.82	-69.61	-34.19	-7.56
26. Singapore	-	-	-53.61	-34.36	-46.58	-35.59	27.40	-	-18.87	-26.03
27. South Korea	-	-	-	57.87	30.07	25.78	29.98	23.71	21.07	31.41
28. Spain	20.34	-	6.96	17.23	23.44	40.87	34.48	22.66	8.34	21.79
29. Sweden	40.50	-	27.31	48.39	58.05	64.91	67.44	40.86	33.13	47.57
30. Switzerland	-	-	-	-	-	-	-	54.47	54.36	54.42
31. Taiwan	-	-	-	-	-	-	-	-	12.65	12.65
32. Thailand	-	-	-	-	-	-	-	-17.84	-19.25	-18.54
33. Venezuela	-	-	-	-	-	26.14	24.72	-	-	24.72
34. Yugoslavia	-	-	-37.52	-95.46	-47.75	-	-	-	-	-46.72
Average	2.68	33.04	-8.84	3.56	11.83	14.97	9.86	8.20	-0.39	6.63

Note: The currency is overvalued if $r_{ct} > 0$; undervalued if $r_{ct} < 0$; and at parity if $r_{ct} = 0$. The grand average of 6.63 per cent overvaluation against the US dollar is derived by dividing the sum of the individual observations by the total number of observations in the sample. This figure does not equal the average of either the cross-sectional or intertemporal averages, as the number of observations for each year and country are irregular over the entire sample.

58

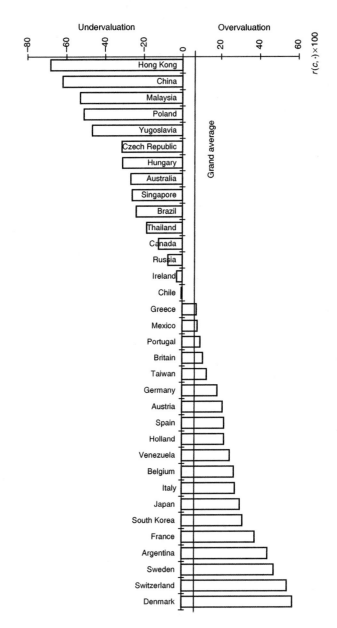

Figure 3.2 Valuation of currencies, 1986–94 averages

Table 3.2 Tests of domestic currency valuation relative to the US dollar, 1986–94 averages

Country	Average $r_c \times 100$	Standard error of mean $\times 100$	t-statistic	Level of significance (%)
1. Argentina	44.36	1.09	40.87	0.1
2. Australia	−26.73	4.65	−5.74	0.1
3. Austria	20.97	–	–	N/A
4. Belgium	26.91	3.61	7.45	0.1
5. Brazil	−23.93	16.48	−1.45	–
6. Britain	11.65	4.40	2.65	5
7. Canada	−12.40	4.25	−2.92	5
8. Chile	−0.48	–	–	N/A
9. China	−61.88	10.98	−5.63	5
10. Czech Republic	−31.38	–	–	N/A
11. Denmark	57.17	3.09	18.48	0.1
12. France	37.74	2.84	13.30	0.1
13. Germany	18.25	2.85	6.40	0.1
14. Greece	7.30	–	–	N/A
15. Holland	21.80	2.24	9.73	0.1
16. Hong Kong	−68.29	3.90	−17.51	0.1
17. Hungary	−31.05	3.14	−9.90	0.1
18. Ireland	−2.89	3.16	−0.92	–
19. Italy	27.48	4.18	6.57	0.1
20. Japan	30.02	4.89	6.14	0.1
21. Malaysia	−52.87	3.38	−15.62	1
22. Mexico	7.82	3.17	2.47	–
23. Poland	−50.95	–	–	N/A
24. Portugal	9.32	–	–	N/A
25. Russia	−7.56	46.22	−0.16	–
26. Singapore	−26.03	10.09	−2.58	5
27. South Korea	31.41	5.48	5.73	1
28. Spain	21.79	4.12	5.28	0.1
29. Sweden	47.57	5.21	9.13	0.1
30. Switzerland	54.42	0.06	978.96	0.1
31. Taiwan	12.65	–	–	N/A
32. Thailand	−18.54	0.71	−26.23	1
33. Venezuela	24.72	–	–	N/A
34. Yugoslavia	−46.72	18.50	−2.52	10
All countries: $r(.,.) \times 100$	6.63	3.00	2.21	5

Note: The t-statistic for each country is derived by dividing the average over- or under-valuation of the domestic currency, in the first column, by its standard error, in the second column. The level of significance in the last column shows the probability of incorrectly rejecting the null hypothesis of a zero average. Where '–' is indicated, the null hypothesis cannot be rejected at any level less than 10 per cent.

intertemporal averages for each country. As can be seen, the currencies of Brazil, Ireland, Mexico and Russia are insignificantly different from parity. All other currencies are either significantly over- or undervalued against the US dollar: the Yugoslavia dinar is significantly undervalued at the 10 per cent level, while the currencies of Britain, Canada, China and Singapore are significantly different from parity at the 5 per cent level. Malaysia, South Korea and Thailand are significantly different from parity at the 1 per cent level, while the remaining currencies are significantly different at the 0.1 per cent level.

The results for Brazil and Russia, especially, provide a strong case for using averages. Although these currencies are two of the most volatile (with standard errors of the mean of 16 and 46 per cent respectively) their alternating positions against the US dollar, from one year to the next, tend to cancel out over time the deviations from parity. Finally, the *t*-statistic for the entire sample indicates that the currencies, averaged over time and countries, deviate significantly from parity at the 5 per cent level.

Figure 3.3 plots for each year the cross-country averages, $r_{.t}$, from the last row of Table 3.1. The US dollar appears overvalued in 1988

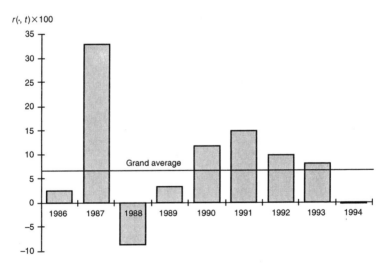

Figure 3.3 Valuation of currencies: annual cross-country averages, 1986–94

Table 3.3 Tests of world currency valuations relative to the US dollar: annual cross-country averages, 1986–94

Statistic	Year									All years $r._{,.} \times 100$
	1986	1987	1988	1989	1990	1991	1992	1993	1994	
Average $r._{,t} \times 100$	2.68	33.04	−8.84	3.56	11.83	14.97	9.86	8.20	−0.39	6.63
Standard error of mean × 100	9.23	7.40	8.96	10.06	10.03	8.88	10.10	7.86	6.37	3.00
t-statistic	0.29	4.46	−0.99	0.35	1.18	1.69	0.98	1.04	−0.06	2.21
Level of significance (%)	–	1	–	–	–	–	–	–	–	5

Note: The t-statistic for each year is derived by dividing the average over- or undervaluation of the domestic currency, in the first row, by its standard error, in the second row. The level of significance in the last row shows the probability of incorrectly rejecting the null hypothesis of a zero average. Where '–' is indicated, the null hypothesis cannot be rejected at any level less than 10 per cent.

and 1994, although not by much in the latter year. The dollar is undervalued in all other years. Results of the t-tests in Table 3.3 seem to imply that the over- or undervaluation of each currency, with respect to the US dollar, tends to offset one another on an annual basis. With the exception of 1987, when the US dollar is significantly overvalued (at the 1 per cent level), it appears that the US dollar is more or less at parity in each year.[6]

Geographic effects

In Figure 3.4, the countries are classified according to regional groupings, namely the Americas, Western and Central Europe, Eastern Europe, East Asia and ASEAN-Oceania. Broadly speaking, it appears that the high-growth, developing economies in the ASEAN-Oceania and Eastern Europe regions are generally undervalued against the US, while the currencies of developed countries in Western and Central Europe, along with those of the highly industrialized East Asian countries of Taiwan, Japan and South Korea, are overvalued.

Table 3.4 tests for parity by region. The figures indicate that except for Western and Central Europe, all other regions are, on average,

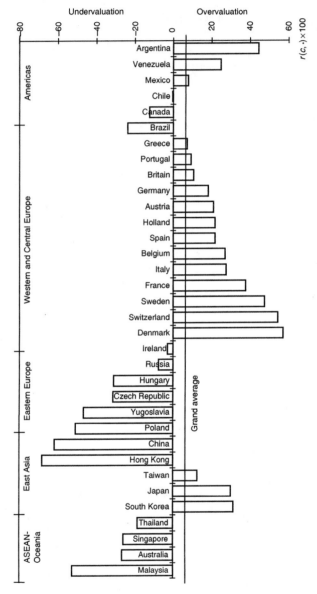

Figure 3.4 Valuation of currencies: regional groups, 1986–94 averages

Table 3.4 Tests of domestic currency valuation relative to the US dollar by region, 1986–94 averages

Region/Country	Average $r_{c,} \times 100$	Standard error of mean $\times 100$	t-statistic	Level of significance (%)
Americas				
1. Argentina	44.36	1.09	40.87	0.1
2. Brazil	−23.93	16.48	−1.45	–
3. Canada	−12.40	4.25	−2.92	5
4. Venezuela	24.72	–	–	N/A
5. Chile	−0.48	–	–	N/A
6. Mexico	7.82	3.17	2.47	–
Region	−1.16	6.50	−0.18	–
Western and Central Europe				
1. Austria	20.97	–	–	N/A
2. Belgium	26.91	3.61	7.45	0.1
3. Britain	11.65	4.40	2.65	5
4. Denmark	57.17	3.09	18.48	0.1
5. Germany	18.25	2.85	6.40	0.1
6. Greece	7.30	–	–	N/A
7. France	37.74	2.84	13.30	0.1
8. Holland	21.80	2.24	9.73	0.1
9. Ireland	−2.89	3.16	−0.92	–
10. Italy	27.48	4.18	6.57	0.1
11. Portugal	9.32	–	–	N/A
12. Spain	21.79	4.12	5.28	0.1
13. Sweden	47.57	5.21	9.13	0.1
14. Switzerland	54.42	0.06	978.96	0.1
Region	26.70	2.02	13.20	0.1
Eastern Europe				
1. Czech Republic	−31.38	–	–	N/A
2. Hungary	−31.05	3.14	−9.90	0.1
3. Poland	−50.95	–	–	N/A
4. Russia	−7.56	46.22	−0.16	–
5. Yugoslavia	−46.72	18.50	−2.52	10
Region	−28.75	15.59	−1.84	10
East Asia				
1. China	−61.88	10.98	−5.63	5
2. Hong Kong	−68.29	3.90	−17.51	0.1
3. Japan	30.02	4.89	6.14	0.1
4. South Korea	31.41	5.48	5.73	1
5. Taiwan	12.65	–	–	N/A
Region	−11.18	9.82	−1.14	–

Table 3.4 Continued

Region/Country	Average $r_{c,} \times 100$	Standard error of mean $\times 100$	t-statistic	Level of significance (%)
ASEAN-Oceania				
1. Australia	−26.73	4.65	−5.74	0.1
2. Malaysia	−52.87	3.38	−15.62	1
3. Singapore	−26.03	10.09	−2.58	5
4. Thailand	−18.54	0.71	−26.23	1
Region	−28.36	4.51	−6.28	0.1

Note: The t-statistic for each country is derived by dividing the average over- or under-valuation of the domestic currency, in the first column, by its standard error, in the second column. The level of significance in the last column shows the probability of incorrectly rejecting the null hypothesis of a zero average. Where '–' is indicated, the null hypothesis cannot be rejected at any level less than 10 per cent.

undervalued against the US. The Western and Central European currencies are significantly overvalued at the 0.1 per cent level. East European currencies are the most volatile, with a standard error of mean of approximately 16 per cent for the region, followed by East Asia where the standard error of mean is 10 per cent. The currencies of ASEAN-Oceania and Eastern Europe are undervalued by about 28 per cent, and the deviations for both regions are significant. The null hypothesis of PPP does hold, however, for the Americas and East Asia.

Test statistics within the regional groupings indicate that the majority of the Western and Central European currencies deviate significantly from parity at the 0.1 per cent level. Only Ireland is at parity with the US. In the Americas group, parity with the US is achieved by Mexico and Brazil, while Canada, surprisingly, deviates from its North American neighbour at the 5 per cent level.[7] All the ASEAN-Oceania currencies are significantly undervalued.

The above findings could perhaps be explained to some extent by Frankel and Wei's (1993) research into the existence of currency blocs, in which they suggest that currency movements are influenced by dominant economies within the selected trade blocs. For instance, the deutschmark appears to dominate the determination of currency values in Europe, while the US dollar is most influential in the Americas. However, Frankel and Wei (1995) show that while there is some evidence of increased Japanese yen influence over the other Asian currencies since the early 1980s, the US dollar appears to be the more dominant currency in this region.

Further tests of Big Mac PPP

In the previous section, we used t-tests to investigate whether departures from PPP are significant, and find that the parity condition generally holds across countries and over time. We now conduct regression-based tests to corroborate our results. Both time-series and average data are used to test for the relationship between actual and implied exchange rates.

Consider the following relationship between the actual exchange rate in country c and year t (S_{ct}) and the corresponding price ratio $p_{ct} = P_{ct}/P_t^*$:

$$S_{ct} = a + b \cdot p_{ct} \tag{3.3}$$

The PPP hypothesis implies a zero intercept term and a unit slope coefficient $(a = 0, \ b = 1)$. The two hypotheses are separately tested using the t-statistic, while the joint hypothesis uses the F-test. Initially, we estimate model (3.3) for each year, using the cross-country data. Additionally, we also estimate a logarithmic version, with both sets of results presented in the first panel of Table 3.5:

$$\log S_{ct} = \alpha + \beta \log p_{ct} \tag{3.4}$$

Looking at the adjusted R^2 figures of the linear model (3.3), there appears to be a significant relationship between the implied and actual exchange rates on a year-by-year basis. Apart from 1989 and 1992, the adjusted R^2 is well over 90 per cent for each year of the sample period.[8] Furthermore, with the exception of 1994, all the intercept terms are not significantly different from zero. However, the majority of the slope coefficients are statistically different from 1 at the 0.1 per cent level, except for 1988 and 1992. The respective F-statistics indicate a rejection of the joint hypothesis of a zero intercept and unit slope, at the 0.1 per cent level of significance, for all years other than 1988 and 1992. On the basis of these results with the linear model, it appears that short-term PPP is achieved only in 1988 and 1992.

Table 3.5 Regression results: exchange rates and prices, 1986–94 (standard errors in parentheses)

Data/Year/Model	Number of observations	Intercept (I)	t-statistic I=0	Level of significance (%)	Slope (S)	t-statistic S=1	Level of significance (%)	Adjusted R²	Standard error	F-statistic I=0 and S=1	Level of significance (%)
I. Cross-country											
1986 Linear	14	1.815 (1.844)	0.984	–	0.708 (0.024)	–12.235	0.1	0.985	6.135	88.3	0.1
Logarithmic	14	0.124 (0.118)	1.050	–	0.915 (0.046)	–1.835	10	0.968	0.318	1.734	–
1987 Linear	8	0.162 (0.479)	0.338	–	0.650 (0.001)	–532.060	0.1	1.000	1.261	163 692.0	0.1
Logarithmic	8	–0.226 (0.087)	–2.580	5	0.953 (0.026)	–1.784	–	0.995	0.183	14.665	5
1988 Linear	16	3.767 (32.601)	0.116	–	1.069 (0.077)	0.892	–	0.927	119.700	0.5	–
Logarithmic	16	0.180 (0.116)	1.553	–	0.958 (0.035)	–1.217	–	0.980	0.353	1.242	–
1989 Linear	17	–200.350 (216.910)	–0.924	–	2.207 (0.223)	5.421	0.1	0.859	817.970	15.7	0.1
Logarithmic	17	–0.010 (0.145)	–0.072	–	0.991 (0.037)	–0.250	–	0.978	0.427	0.090	–
1990 Linear	18	4.864 (3.481)	1.398	–	0.703 (0.007)	–40.799	0.1	0.998	13.756	936.4	0.1
Logarithmic	18	–0.014 (0.135)	–0.101	–	0.953 (0.041)	–1.147	–	0.969	0.422	1.366	–
1991 Linear	19	1.550 (2.390)	0.649	–	0.773 (0.006)	–40.765	0.1	0.999	9.677	951.9	0.1
Logarithmic	19	–0.063 (0.128)	–0.488	–	0.964 (0.039)	–0.942	–	0.972	0.388	1.856	–
1992 Linear	22	–0.179 (40.005)	–0.005	–	0.900 (0.068)	–1.477	–	0.893	171.720	1.3	–
Logarithmic	22	–0.073 (0.154)	–0.472	–	0.990 (0.042)	–0.229	–	0.964	0.485	0.481	–
1993 Linear	24	13.379 (18.516)	0.723	–	0.814 (0.003)	–69.248	0.1	1.000	88.346	2515.9	0.1
Logarithmic	24	–0.048 (0.113)	–0.423	–	0.987 (0.029)	–0.437	–	0.981	0.392	0.621	–
1994 Linear	31	–121.520 (61.863)	–1.964	10	1.651 (0.025)	25.996	0.1	0.993	332.980	350.1	0.1
Logarithmic	31	–0.028 (0.103)	–0.277	–	1.010 (0.025)	0.406	–	0.982	0.360	0.084	–
II. Cross-country/time-series											
Linear	169	55.240 (73.511)	0.752	–	0.940 (0.026)	–2.311	5	0.888	942.090	2.7	10
Logarithmic	162	–0.017 (0.042)	–0.411	–	0.981 (0.012)	–1.620	–	0.977	0.388	3.777	5
III. Average over time											
Linear	34	–96.766 (201.620)	–0.480	–	1.414 (0.072)	5.784	0.1	0.922	1123.100	17.6	0.1
Logarithmic	34	–0.018 (0.094)	–0.190	–	1.001 (0.024)	0.037	–	0.982	0.347	0.033	–

When the logarithmic model (3.4) is used, all three hypotheses cannot be rejected for any one year, except for 1986 and 1987. We find the slope coefficient for 1986 to be significantly different from unity at the 10 per cent level. The intercept term for 1987 is different from zero at the 5 per cent level of significance, while the joint hypothesis is also rejected at the 5 per cent level of significance for that year. Overall, the logarithmic model appears to model short-term PPP very well, with the year-by-year regression results in the first panel of Table 3.5 showing strong support for its existence.

Next, we pool the data over time and across countries,[9] and the results are presented in the second panel of Table 3.5. Consistent with the majority of the year-by-year results for the linear model, the intercept term is not significantly different from zero, whilst the slope coefficient differs significantly from unity at the 5 per cent level. However, the joint hypothesis, in this instance, cannot be rejected at any level of significance. As with the individual-year results, the pooled results for the logarithmic model also show a marked improvement relative to the linear model, with the adjusted R^2 increasing to 98 per cent from 89 per cent. In this case, both the null hypotheses of a zero intercept and unity in the slope coefficient, when taken separately, cannot be rejected. However, the joint hypothesis is rejected at the 5 per cent level of significance.

Subsequently, let $S_c = (1/T) \cdot \sum_{t=1}^{T} S_{ct}$ and $p_c = (1/T) \cdot \sum_{t=1}^{T} p_{ct}$ be the average exchange rate and relative price for country c. We now use these averages in the cross-country regressions:

$$S_c = a + b \cdot p_c. \tag{3.5}$$

and

$$\log S_c = \alpha + \beta \log p_c. \tag{3.6}$$

where the logarithmic averages are analogously defined as $\log S_c = (1/T) \cdot \sum_{t=1}^{T} \log S_{ct}$ and $\log p_c = (1/T) \cdot \sum_{t=1}^{T} \log p_{ct}$. The estimates of these equations are given in the third panel of Table 3.5. We see that the results for the linear model (3.5) show an improvement in the adjusted R^2 of 92 per cent relative to the 'pooled data' figure of 89 per cent, obtained from the equation (3.3) model. However, the null hypothesis for the slope coefficient is still rejected, this time at the 0.1 per cent level. Furthermore, the F-statistic shows that the joint hypothesis is rejected at the 0.1 per cent level of significance. Using the logarithmic model in (3.6), the adjusted R^2 further

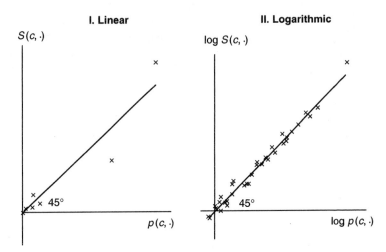

Figure 3.5   Exchange rates and prices: country averages, 1986–94

improves to 98 per cent. The intercept and slope coefficient are not significantly different from zero and unity, respectively, while the joint hypothesis for the slope and intercept also cannot be rejected. Figure 3.5 gives scatterplots of the 'averaged' data.

In conclusion, it appears that PPP holds in logarithmic form as a long-run proposition; that is, when the data are averaged over time. This result is intuitively appealing in that logarithmic transformations reduce the relative magnitude of outliers in the data, while the averaging process decreases the effects of short-run volatility of exchange rate fluctuations. Also, note that this long-run result agrees with prior findings, as discussed previously.

Relative parity

Previously, we employed PPP in terms of levels, $\log S_{ct} = \log(P_{ct}/P_t^*)$, which is also known as *absolute PPP*. The *relative* version is in first differences:

$$\Delta \log S_{ct} = \Delta \log p_{ct}$$

where $p_{ct} = P_{ct}/P_t^*$, as before. Thus, $\Delta \log S_{ct} \times 100$ is approximately the percentage change in the actual exchange rate, while $\Delta \log p_{ct} \times 100$ is approximately the percentage change in the implied exchange rate.

The economic distinction between the two parity versions relates to impediments to PPP such as trade barriers, differential taxes, and so on, which may be more or less constant over time. When we take first differences, these country-specific factors drop out. For instance, if the price of food is always relatively more expensive in a particular country, then the use of price changes will eliminate this feature from the data. Similarly, the size of the currency denominations would be of little significance. In effect, the use of changes over time 'standardizes' the exchange rates and prices across countries. Furthermore, the use of first differences would account for the $I(1)$ property of exchange rates.[10]

In this section, we analyse the performance of relative PPP with the Big Mac data. We define the actual change in currency c from year $t-1$ to t as $\Delta \log S_{ct} = \log S_{ct} - \log S_{c,t-1}$. If currency c depreciates (appreciates), then $\Delta \log S_{ct} > 0$ (<0). The change in the corresponding implied exchange rate is $\Delta \log p_{ct} = \log p_{ct} - \log p_{c,t-1}$. Note that as $p_{ct} = P_{ct}/P_t^*$, $\Delta \log p_{ct} = \pi_{ct} - \pi_t^*$, where $\pi_{ct} = \log P_{ct} - \log P_{c,t-1}$ is the change in the domestic price and $\pi_t^* = \log P_t^* - \log P_{t-1}^*$ is the change in the US price. Where the price of a Big Mac in country c increases more (less) than the US, $\Delta \log p_{ct} > 0$ (<0), implying a depreciation (appreciation) in the implied exchange rate. The actual country and year-by-year averages are calculated as $\Delta \log S_{c.} = (1/T_c) \cdot \sum_{t=1}^{T_c} \Delta \log S_{ct}$ and $\Delta \log S_{.t} = (1/N_t) \cdot \sum_{c=1}^{N_t} \Delta \log S_{ct}$, respectively, while the implied averages for the same are calculated as $\Delta \log p_{c.} = (1/T_c) \cdot \sum_{t=1}^{T_c} \Delta \log p_{ct}$ and $\Delta \log p_{.t} = (1/N_t) \cdot \sum_{c=1}^{N_t} \Delta \log p_{ct}$, respectively.

The results of the regression of $\Delta \log S_{ct}$ on $\Delta \log p_{ct}$ show that the adjusted R^2 of the regression is approximately 90 per cent, while the intercept and slope coefficient are not significantly different from zero and unity, respectively. We also find that the joint hypothesis of a zero intercept and unit slope cannot be rejected at any level of significance. This indicates that the changes in the actual series are not significantly different from the implied ones. Figure 3.6 shows the observations to be closely distributed along the 45 degree line. Overall, these results appear to provide strong support for the use of Big Mac prices for making PPP comparisons.

Possible causes of deviations from parity

Our findings to this point indicate that Big Mac PPP generally holds for our sample countries, both on a year-by-year basis, and averaged

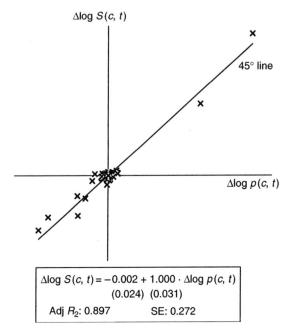

Figure 3.6   Exchange rate movements: cross-country/time-series, 1986–94

over nine years. However, our results are not without exception. In several instances the exchange rates have been found to deviate significantly from parity. We will now explore the different possibilities as to how these deviations could occur in the context of our research.

The theory of PPP assumes that there are no barriers to trade. It has been long recognized that such barriers prevent arbitrage from taking place and lead to departures from parity.[11] In our case, these market imperfections would be further augmented by cost differentials as a result of comparative advantage between countries within the Big Mac production chain. Although the Big Macs are made locally, the same may not be true for each individual ingredient required to make it, for example meat and wheat are produced cheaply in Australia and the US, but labour in these countries costs more than, say, the developing countries such as Malaysia and Thailand.[12]

Big Mac prices could also be distorted by high taxes in countries such as Denmark and Sweden, and inflated property costs in Hong

Kong, Japan and Singapore, which could exaggerate the degree of departure from parity for these currencies. However, if it could be argued that the pricing of Big Macs does incorporate these costs, then they would be ideal measures since these costs would presumably apply to the economy as a whole.

The 'status symbol' argument suggests that in certain countries, fast-food chains in general, and the McDonald's franchise in particular, are rarities and are thus able to command a monopoly premium over other commodities. This is not the case in the US where intense competition from other fast-food chains would serve to keep margins slim. It has often been held that the failure of the law of one price is due, in large part, to systematic attempts by firms operating in international markets to stabilize destination market prices when nominal exchange rates change, in order to protect market share. Firms are said to 'price to market' when they charge different local prices across export markets to reflect the particular local competitive situation.[13] Thus, any exchange rate movement is absorbed by altering the home currency export price.[14]

The deviations from parity could partly be due to the exchange rates themselves. Institutional intervention in foreign exchange rate markets by central banks results in a 'managed' float whereby rates can be artificially held away from their underlying economic fundamental values.

Another important reason for deviations from PPP is the existence of productivity differences between countries. For example, if international productivity differences are greater in the production of traded goods than non-traded goods, then the currency of rich countries, which have higher overall productivity levels, will appear overvalued in PPP terms (Balassa, 1964). The *productivity bias hypothesis*, as this is commonly known, will be investigated in the next two sections.

Is the Big Mac all tradeable?

According to Harrod (1939, p. 71):

> the rate at which currencies exchange against each other should normally be that rate which causes each when converted into the other to purchase the same quantity of goods in the land of the currency into which it has converted as it purchases at home.

He sees this definition as holding true for traded goods (hereafter T) only, as the prices of these goods are purely the effect of exchange rate movements. Accordingly, these prices should not vary outside the limits set by transportation costs and tariffs. Harrod argues that PPP no longer holds once non-traded goods (hereafter N) are taken into account, since they are not expected to have the same prices in different countries except under special circumstances. Balassa (1964) subsequently formalizes Harrod's exposition by looking at deviations from PPP in the context of productivity biases. He finds that marked productivity differentials in T between 'rich' and 'poor' countries, along with wage equalization within each economy, cause the prices of N in terms of T to be higher in the richer economies. We will use this approach as a basis for slicing the Big Mac into its T and N components.

Clements and Frenkel (1980) take the price level to be a linear homogeneous (Cobb–Douglas) function of the prices of N, P_N, and T, P_T, with weight α given to N:

$$P = P_N^{\alpha} \cdot P_T^{1-\alpha} \tag{3.7}$$

where $0 < \alpha < 1$. As this implies that $P = P_T \left(\dfrac{P_N}{P_T}\right)^{\alpha}$, it follows that

$$P_T = P \left(\frac{P_T}{P_N}\right)^{\alpha} \tag{3.8}$$

Similarly, for the foreign country (denoted by an asterisk),

$$P_T^{\star} = P^{\star} \left(\frac{P_T^{\star}}{P_N^{\star}}\right)^{\alpha^{\star}} \tag{3.9}$$

If PPP applies to T only, then $S = P_T/P_T^{\star}$, and it follows that

$$P_T = S \cdot P_T^{\star} \tag{3.10}$$

Substituting (3.8) and (3.9) into (3.10), we obtain

$$P \left(\frac{P_T}{P_N}\right)^{\alpha} = S \cdot P^{\star} \left(\frac{P_T^{\star}}{P_N^{\star}}\right)^{\alpha^{\star}}$$

so that

$$S = \frac{(P_T/P_N)^\alpha}{(P_T^*/P_N^*)^{\alpha^*}} \cdot \frac{P}{P^*} \tag{3.11}$$

Consider a two-country world, where one country is rich and the other poor. Let the rich country be more productive in the production of both T and N. Although this country has an absolute advantage in both goods, it is plausible to postulate that it is relatively more productive in T. The reason lies in the nature of N, which have large service components and are labour-intensive. Thus, productivity improvements are more difficult in these areas. Consequently, the relatively higher productivity of T in the rich country means that their relative price will be cheaper in the rich country (in terms of N). This is Balassa's argument.

Since N enters into the calculation of PPP via the overall price level, but does not directly affect exchange rates, the currency of the richer country will appear to be 'overvalued'. Looking at equation (3.11), we can see that the $(P_T/P_N)^\alpha$ term becomes smaller, on the basis of a simple PPP calculation, as T becomes relatively cheaper to N in the rich country. As the numerator decreases relative to the denominator in the term $(P_T/P_N)^\alpha/(P_T^*/P_N^*)^{\alpha^*}$, this term falls. The result is a greater 'gap' between PPP (as represented by P/P^*) and the equilibrium exchange rate, S. Thus, the currency of the country with higher productivity levels appears overvalued in PPP terms if the PPP value of the exchange rate is defined merely as P/P^*.

Clements and Semudram (1983) analyse this relationship between the relative prices of T and N and gross domestic product (GDP) per capita by estimating the following equation:

$$\log\left(\frac{P_T}{P_N}\right) = \lambda + \phi \log GDP \tag{3.12}$$

They use the price of haircuts in 24 countries to measure the price of N. They find a strong association between the price of a haircut and the GDP, and estimate ϕ in (3.12) as being equal to 0.256 with a standard error of 0.061. Accordingly, the income elasticity of the relative price of T is about 0.260. Furthermore, their analysis of the relationship between the relative price and per capita GDP within nine selected countries through time shows that the income elasticities of P_T/P_N are all negative and significant. Their finding that N become relatively more expensive with increasing income supports the above argument.

We rewrite (3.12) for the foreign economy as

$$\log\left(\frac{P_T^*}{P_N^*}\right) = \lambda^* + \phi^* \log GDP^* \tag{3.13}$$

and express (3.11) in logarithmic form:

$$\log S = \alpha \log\left(\frac{P_T}{P_N}\right) - \alpha^* \log\left(\frac{P_T^*}{P_N^*}\right) + \log\left(\frac{P}{P^*}\right) \tag{3.14}$$

If we substitute (3.12) and (3.13) for $\log(P_T/P_N)$ and $\log(P_T^*/P_N^*)$ respectively, in equation (3.14), we then obtain:

$$\log S = \gamma + \beta \log GDP - \beta^* \log GDP^* + \log\left(\frac{P}{P^*}\right) \tag{3.15}$$

where $\gamma = \alpha\lambda - \alpha^*\lambda^*$, $\beta = \alpha\phi$ and $\beta^* = \alpha^*\phi^*$. Assuming for expository purposes that $\alpha = \alpha^*$ and $\phi = \phi^*$, then $\beta = \beta^*$, so that (3.15) becomes

$$\log S = \gamma + \beta \log\left(\frac{GDP}{GDP^*}\right) + \log\left(\frac{P}{P^*}\right) \tag{3.16}$$

As in our earlier discussion on the valuation of currencies, we define the over/undervaluation of the currency in (3.2) as

$$r \equiv \log\frac{P}{P^*} - \log S$$

so that $r > 0$ (< 0) implies that the currency is over-undervalued. (The negative of r is the conventional definition of the real exchange rate.) We can thus take the term $\log(P/P^*)$ to the left-hand side of equation (3.16) and rewrite it as

$$r = \gamma' + \beta' \log\left(\frac{GDP}{GDP^*}\right) \tag{3.17}$$

where $\gamma' = -\gamma$ and $\beta' = -\beta$. As the coefficient $\beta = \alpha\phi$, with $0 < \alpha < 1$ and $\phi < 0$, we expect $\beta < 0$ and $\beta' > 0$. Consequently, as the country becomes poorer, the ratio GDP/GDP^* falls towards zero and $\log(GDP/GDP^*)$ becomes more negative; the term $\beta' \log(GDP/GDP^*)$ also becomes more negative, so that r falls and the currency of the country becomes more undervalued. The estimates of equation (3.17) are given in Table 3.6.[15]

To interpret these estimates, suppose that the GDP per capita of country c is US\$1000, and that of the foreign economy (in this case the US) is US\$18 000, so that

$$\frac{GDP}{GDP^*} = \frac{1}{18} = 0.056, \quad \log\left(\frac{GDP}{GDP^*}\right) = -2.890$$

Thus, country c is approximately 95 per cent less affluent than the US. We use the Table 3.6 estimates of $\hat{\gamma}' = 0.259$ and $\hat{\beta}' = 0.240$ to calculate the estimated value of currency c:

$$\hat{r}_c = 0.259 + 0.240 \cdot (-2.890)$$

$$= -0.435$$

that is, the currency of country c is undervalued by approximately 44 per cent.

Recall that one of the basic (or structural) parameters of this model is α, the share of non-tradeables in total costs. As the coefficient $\beta' = -\alpha\phi$, we can obtain an estimate of α given estimates of β' and ϕ, the income elasticity of the relative price of tradeables. We use Clements and Semudram's (1983) estimate $\hat{\phi} = -0.256$ to derive α:

$$\hat{\alpha} \equiv \frac{-\hat{\beta}'}{\hat{\phi}} = \frac{-0.238}{-0.256} = 0.930$$

Table 3.6 Regression results: currency valuation and GDP—cross-country/time-series, 1986–94 (standard errors in parentheses)

Intercept coefficient γ'	0.259	(0.026)
Coefficient of relative GDP β'	0.240	(0.023)
Adjusted R^2	0.415	
Standard error of estimate	0.266	

Thus, the non-traded component in a Big Mac accounts for approximately 93 per cent of its cost. This figure appears reasonable given the prominence of wages, rents and other overheads in the cost of a Big Mac.

Improving the Big Mac Index: the No-Frills Index

As previously discussed, PPP theory needs to be extended to take account of N. Our calculations in the previous section indicate that, on average, N account for approximately 93 per cent of the hamburger prices. Since these goods play only a very small part in determining exchange rates, they should be excluded in a more sophisticated PPP calculation. We pursue this idea in this section by introducing the No-Frills Index (NFI) in which N are excluded from the Big Mac Index (BMI).

Equation (3.10) is the PPP condition applied to T. We write this in logarithmic form:

$$\log S = \log P_T - \log P_T^*$$

$$= f(\log P, \log GDP) - f^*(\log P^*, \log GDP^*)$$

$$= g\left(\log\frac{P}{P^*}, \log\frac{GDP}{GDP^*}\right) \tag{3.18}$$

In the above, the second line reflects equations (3.7) and (3.12) and their foreign-country counterparts. The third line invokes (1) a homogeneity assumption that prices at home *relative* to those abroad affect the exchange rate; and (2) an assumption that the relevant parameter values are identical in the two countries, $\alpha = \alpha^*$ and $\phi = \phi^*$, in the notation of the previous section.

Once we have an estimate of the parameters of the function $g(\cdot, \cdot)$ in (3.18), we can estimate the NFI:

$$\log \hat{S} = \hat{g}\left(\log\frac{P}{P^*}, \log\frac{GDP}{GDP^*}\right)$$

This index is computed as

$$\log \hat{S} \equiv \log S - \hat{\varepsilon}$$

where S is the actual exchange rate and ε is the residual from the productivity bias equation (3.17).[16] Another way of visualizing the

NFI is that it incorporates the systematic relationship between departures from parity according to the BMI and GDP; this relationship is the productivity bias equation (3.17).

The NFI is presented in Table A3.1, in Appendix 3.2. As expected, we see from column 5 of the table that the NFI is not significantly different from the actual exchange rate. This is in contrast with the results in columns 4 and 5, which respectively show the actual exchange rates and the NFI to be significantly different from the BMI at the 0.1 per cent level.

The last entry of column 6 of Table A3.1 reveals that the mean of the excess of the BMI over its No-Frills counterpart is about 10 per cent. In other words, the BMI undervalues currencies by 10 per cent, on average. Consequently, if *The Economist* magazine wishes to make some rough adjustments to its BMI to allow for the productivity bias, a simple approach would be to add 10 per cent to its estimates of currency values, especially for the poorest countries.

Conclusion

The Economist magazine is considered the most influential and prestigious financial newspaper in the world. In view of its well-known breezy style which has been described as 'simplify and then exaggerate', one suspects that when the Editor first introduced the Big Mac Index in 1986, it was a somewhat tongue-in-cheek contribution to what is perhaps the most widely-researched and debated doctrine in international finance. Nine years later, the Big Mac Index is still going strong, and is now widely cited and used by academics and practitioners alike. Given the competitive nature of publishing, one would assume that the survival of the Index is based on some intrinsic merit and usefulness of the measure in judging the long-term value of currencies.

Our test results demonstrate that the Big Mac Index is surprisingly accurate in tracking exchange rates over the longer term. The regression tests indicate that purchasing power parity holds with the Big Mac Index over a nine-year horizon, which is consistent with previous findings. However, that is not to say that the currencies of all individual countries for all years are at parity. Geographic influences appear to play a part in those instances where deviations from parity occur. For example, the currencies of developing Asian and East European countries are consistently undervalued, while the currencies of the industrialized economies are overvalued on average.

The versatility of the Big Mac Index notwithstanding, we were still able to further improve on it by taking into account the existence of productivity bias between countries. According to the productivity bias hypothesis, services are relatively cheaper in poorer countries, and because these goods have little, if any, role in determining exchange rates, standard PPP calculations which include services seem to imply that the currencies of these countries are systematically undervalued. In other words, these deviations from parity are related to GDP. We have confirmed the existence of productivity bias in the Big Mac Index, and subsequently introduced the No-Frills Index to solve this problem. The new index excludes the non-traded component of Big Mac hamburgers in computing parity. Interestingly, we estimated that this component accounts for as much as 93 per cent of the cost of a Big Mac. Our new results indicate that the No-Frills Index performs even better than the Big Mac Index in tracking exchange rates over the long term, and could be of use to practitioners and policy-makers.

Appendix 3.1: No-Frills Index

Earlier in the chapter, we substituted (3.8) and (3.9) into (3.10) to obtain (3.11), and its logarithmic form in (3.14):

$$\log S = \alpha \log\left(\frac{P_T}{P_N}\right) - \alpha^\star \log\left(\frac{P_T^\star}{P_N^\star}\right) + \log\left(\frac{P}{P^\star}\right)$$

Incorporating (3.12) and (3.13) into (3.14), we obtain (3.16):

$$\log S = \gamma + \beta \log\left(\frac{GDP}{GDP^\star}\right) + \log\left(\frac{P}{P^\star}\right)$$

From (3.17), we know that,

$$r = \gamma' + \beta' \log\left(\frac{GDP}{GDP^\star}\right)$$

where $\gamma' = -\gamma$ and $\beta' = -\beta$. This is equivalent to:

$$r = \hat{\gamma}' + \hat{\beta}' \log\left(\frac{GDP}{GDP^\star}\right) - \varepsilon, \quad \text{or}$$

$$\hat{r} = \hat{\gamma}' + \hat{\beta}' \log\left(\frac{GDP}{GDP^\star}\right) \qquad (3.17')$$

where $\hat{\gamma}'$ and $\hat{\beta}'$ are the regression estimates of γ' and β' respectively; and ε is the regression residual. Since the regression residuals indicate deviations from

PPP, it then follows that they must represent the relative prices of N in the respective economies. Therefore

$$r = \hat{r} - \varepsilon$$

$$\Leftrightarrow \hat{r} = r + \varepsilon$$

Previously, we know from (3.2) that

$$r \equiv \log \frac{P}{P^*} - \log S$$

If we redefine (3.2) as

$$\log S \equiv \log \frac{P}{P^*} - r \tag{3.2'}$$

then, substituting (3.17') into (3.2'), would give:

$$\log S = \log \frac{P}{P^*} - \left[\hat{\gamma}' + \hat{\beta}' \log\left(\frac{GDP}{GDP^*}\right) - \varepsilon \right]$$

$$= \log \frac{P}{P^*} - \left[\hat{\gamma}' + \hat{\beta}' \log\left(\frac{GDP}{GDP^*}\right) \right] + \varepsilon, \quad \text{or}$$

$$\log \;\; = \log\left(\frac{P}{P^*}\right) - \left[\hat{\gamma}' + \hat{\beta}' \log\left(\frac{GDP}{GDP^*}\right) \right]$$

$$= \textit{Conventional Big Mac Index} - \textit{Adjustment for GDP}$$

This yields the following identities:

$$\log S \equiv \log \hat{S} + \varepsilon$$

$$\Leftrightarrow \quad \log \hat{S} \equiv \log S - \varepsilon \qquad \text{Q.E.D.}$$

that is, $\log \hat{S}$ could be derived by subtracting from $\log S$ (actual) the residuals from the estimates of equation (3.17).

Alternatively, we could substitute (3.2') into the identity, so that

$$\log \hat{S} \equiv \left[\log\frac{P}{P^*} - r \right] - \varepsilon$$

$$= \log\frac{P}{P^*} - (r + \varepsilon)$$

$$= \log\frac{P}{P^*} - \hat{r}$$

where $\log \hat{S}$ is calculated by subtracting the estimated currency under- or over-valuation from the implied exchange rate (logarithmic).

80

Appendix 3.2: The No-Frills Index

Table A3.1 Actual exchange rates, the Big Mac Index and the No-Frills Index

Country	Logarithmic			Logarithmic differences × 100		
	Actual exchange rate (ER) (1)	Big Mac Index (BMI) (2)	No-Frills Index (NFI) (3)	Actual ER-BMI (4) = (1) – (2)	Actual ER-NFI (5) = (1) – (3)	BMI-NFI (6) = (2) – (3)
1986						
Australia	0.49	0.09	−0.02	40.85	51.86	11.01
Belgium	3.74	4.03	3.86	−28.77	−12.12	16.65
Brazil	2.62	2.05	2.57	57.05	5.38	−51.68
Britain	−0.40	−0.37	−0.50	−2.94	9.47	12.42
Canada	0.33	0.17	−0.04	16.38	37.22	20.84
France	1.89	2.33	2.13	−43.75	−23.99	19.76
Germany	0.70	0.98	0.75	−27.52	−4.62	22.91
Holland	0.82	1.00	0.81	−17.65	1.16	18.80
Ireland	−0.30	−0.30	−0.35	0.00	5.33	5.33
Japan	5.04	5.44	5.18	−40.55	−14.43	26.12
Singapore	0.77	0.56	0.52	20.59	24.84	4.26
Spain	4.89	5.09	5.08	−20.34	−19.22	1.12
Sweden	1.93	2.33	2.09	−40.50	−16.35	24.15
1987						
Belgium	3.67	4.03	3.85	−36.29	−18.21	18.08
Britain	−0.39	−0.34	−0.63	−4.32	24.30	28.62
Denmark	1.97	2.60	2.34	−62.55	−36.28	26.28
France	1.84	2.39	2.18	−54.64	−33.72	20.91
Germany	0.64	0.94	0.70	−30.34	−6.36	23.98
Holland	0.76	1.03	0.84	−27.71	−8.54	19.17
Ireland	−0.36	−0.30	−0.37	−5.49	1.53	7.02
Italy	7.20	7.63	7.46	−43.01	−26.20	16.81
1988						
Australia	0.31	−0.20	−0.37	50.59	68.24	17.65
Belgium	3.55	3.63	3.42	−7.90	12.92	20.82
Britain	−0.62	−0.69	−0.89	7.70	27.15	19.45
Canada	0.22	−0.15	−0.40	36.59	61.11	24.51
Denmark	1.85	2.25	1.97	−40.34	−11.65	28.68
France	1.73	1.98	1.74	−25.15	−1.56	23.60
Germany	0.51	0.54	0.28	−3.55	23.01	26.56
Holland	0.62	0.71	0.49	−8.75	12.79	21.54
Ireland	−0.48	−0.67	−0.77	19.53	29.65	10.12
Italy	7.11	7.23	7.03	−11.59	8.16	19.75
Japan	4.82	5.04	4.74	−22.31	8.41	30.72

Table A3.1 Continued

Country	Logarithmic			Logarithmic differences × 100		
	Actual exchange rate (ER) (1)	Big Mac Index (BMI) (2)	No-Frills Index (NFI) (3)	Actual ER-BMI (4) = (1) − (2)	Actual ER-NFI (5) = (1) − (3)	BMI-NFI (6) = (2) − (3)
Singapore	0.69	0.16	0.07	53.61	62.48	8.86
Italy	7.11	7.23	7.03	−11.59	8.16	19.75
Japan	4.82	5.04	4.74	−22.31	8.41	30.72
Singapore	0.69	0.16	0.07	53.61	62.48	8.86
Spain	4.71	4.78	4.70	−6.96	0.72	7.68
Sweden	1.77	2.05	1.76	−27.31	1.35	28.66
Yugoslavia	7.24	6.87	7.51	37.52	−26.78	−64.30
1989						
Australia	0.22	0.04	−0.17	17.59	38.32	20.73
Belgium	3.68	3.81	3.63	−13.04	5.12	18.16
Britain	−0.53	−0.48	−0.66	−4.96	13.01	17.97
Canada	0.17	0.06	−0.20	11.57	37.04	25.48
Denmark	1.99	2.51	2.26	−51.76	−26.79	24.97
France	1.85	2.17	1.96	−31.86	−11.08	20.78
Germany	0.64	0.76	0.52	−11.95	11.28	23.23
Holland	0.76	0.92	0.74	−16.81	1.28	18.10
Ireland	−0.34	−0.45	−0.53	10.38	18.71	8.33
Italy	7.23	7.40	7.22	−16.75	0.85	17.60
Japan	4.89	5.21	4.92	−31.91	−2.86	29.06
Singapore	0.67	0.33	0.22	34.36	45.25	10.89
South Korea	6.50	7.08	7.15	−57.87	−65.36	−7.49
Spain	4.76	4.93	4.86	−17.23	−9.54	7.69
Sweden	1.86	2.34	2.07	−48.39	−20.92	27.47
Yugoslavia	9.11	8.15	8.56	95.46	54.79	−40.67
1990						
Australia	0.28	0.05	−0.14	22.88	42.16	19.28
Belgium	3.55	3.78	3.57	−23.89	−2.14	21.75
Britain	−0.49	−0.45	−0.62	−4.80	12.91	17.71
Canada	0.15	0.00	−0.25	14.84	40.34	25.50
Denmark	1.85	2.45	2.17	−59.63	−31.40	28.23
France	1.73	2.09	1.85	−35.76	−11.78	23.98
Germany	0.52	0.67	0.40	−14.90	11.84	26.74
Holland	0.63	0.87	0.66	−24.00	−2.52	21.49
Ireland	−0.46	−0.53	−0.65	6.56	18.48	11.92
Italy	7.11	7.48	7.26	−36.57	−14.91	21.66
Japan	5.07	5.12	4.87	−5.51	19.88	−5.39
Singapore	0.63	0.17	0.03	46.58	60.29	13.72

Table A3.1 Continued

Country	Logarithmic			Logarithmic differences × 100		
	Actual exchange rate (ER) (1)	Big Mac Index (BMI) (2)	No-Frills Index (NFI) (3)	Actual ER-BMI (4) = (1) − (2)	Actual ER-NFI (5) = (1) − (3)	BMI-NFI (6) = (2) − (3)
South Korea	6.56	6.86	6.92	−30.07	−35.74	−5.67
Spain	4.66	4.90	4.78	−23.44	−11.81	11.63
Sweden	1.81	2.39	2.09	−58.05	−28.19	29.86
1991						
Australia	0.24	0.09	−0.11	15.28	34.75	19.47
Belgium	3.54	3.79	3.57	−25.32	−2.92	22.39
Britain	−0.58	−0.30	−0.50	−27.87	−7.78	20.10
Canada	0.14	0.04	−0.20	10.05	34.06	24.01
Denmark	1.86	2.48	2.19	−61.63	−33.30	28.32
France	1.73	2.08	1.84	−34.78	−10.65	24.13
Germany	0.51	0.65	0.42	−13.43	9.29	22.72
Holland	0.63	0.85	0.63	−21.46	0.41	21.87
Hungary	4.32	3.93	4.14	38.51	17.50	−21.01
Ireland	−0.48	−0.48	−0.60	0.00	12.50	12.50
Italy	7.12	7.38	7.15	−25.57	−2.30	23.27
Japan	4.91	5.13	4.83	−22.46	7.65	30.11
Singapore	0.57	0.22	0.05	35.59	52.26	16.67
South Korea	6.58	6.84	6.86	−25.78	−28.33	−2.55
Spain	4.63	5.04	4.90	−40.87	−27.02	13.85
Sweden	1.80	2.45	2.14	−64.91	−34.08	30.83
1992						
Argentina	−0.01	0.41	0.45	−42.22	−45.89	−3.68
Australia	0.27	0.15	−0.04	12.16	30.56	18.40
Belgium	3.51	3.90	3.67	−38.53	−15.32	23.21
Brazil	7.67	7.46	7.81	21.59	−13.65	−35.24
Britain	−0.56	−0.24	−0.43	−32.64	−13.11	19.53
Canada	0.17	0.23	0.01	−5.72	16.74	22.45
China	1.69	1.06	1.79	63.60	29.97	−73.57
Denmark	1.84	2.52	2.24	−67.72	−39.26	28.46
France	1.71	2.11	1.87	−39.76	−15.52	24.25
Germany	0.49	0.72	0.48	−22.31	1.16	23.48
Holland	0.61	0.89	0.67	−28.22	−5.93	22.30
Hungary	4.38	4.11	4.30	−7.18	7.80	−19.38
Ireland	−0.49	−0.42	−0.55	−7.88	5.27	13.14
Italy	7.12	7.53	7.30	−41.76	−18.04	23.71
Japan	4.89	5.16	4.86	−26.87	3.19	30.06

Table A3.1 Continued

Country	Logarithmic			Logarithmic differences × 100		
	Actual exchange rate (ER) (1)	Big Mac Index (BMI) (2)	No-Frills Index (NFI) (3)	Actual ER-BMI (4) = (1) − (2)	Actual ER-NFI (5) = (1) − (3)	BMI-NFI (6) = (2) − (3)
Russia	4.59	3.28	3.71	131.82	88.12	−43.70
Singapore	0.50	0.77	0.59	−27.40	−8.86	18.54
South Korea	6.66	6.96	6.99	−29.98	−32.93	−2.95
Spain	4.62	4.97	4.82	−34.48	−19.65	14.83
Sweden	1.78	2.45	2.15	−67.44	−37.35	30.09
Venezuela	4.10	4.35	4.56	−24.72	−45.51	−20.79
1993						
Argentina	0.00	0.46	0.48	−45.74	−47.83	−2.08
Australia	0.33	0.07	−0.10	26.16	43.15	16.99
Belgium	3.48	3.87	3.63	−38.75	−15.18	23.58
Brazil	10.22	10.43	10.66	−20.47	−43.44	−22.97
Britain	−0.45	−0.24	−0.41	−21.06	−4.07	16.99
Canada	0.23	0.19	−0.01	4.05	24.48	20.43
China	1.74	1.32	2.01	42.05	−27.40	−69.45
Denmark	1.80	2.42	2.13	−62.22	−33.33	28.89
France	1.68	2.09	1.85	−41.79	−17.47	24.32
Germany	0.46	0.70	0.47	−24.57	−1.04	23.53
Holland	0.57	0.87	0.65	−30.03	−7.44	22.59
Hungary	4.48	4.23	4.41	24.73	6.47	−18.26
Ireland	−0.43	−0.43	−0.55	0.00	12.25	12.25
Italy	7.33	7.59	7.41	−25.94	−7.71	18.23
Japan	4.73	5.14	4.81	−41.43	−8.38	33.05
Malaysia	0.95	0.39	0.61	56.25	34.11	−22.15
Mexico	1.13	1.24	1.41	−10.99	−28.33	−17.34
Russia	6.53	5.83	6.22	69.61	31.25	−38.35
South Korea	6.68	6.92	6.94	−23.71	−25.90	−2.19
Spain	4.74	4.96	4.84	−22.66	−10.82	11.85
Sweden	2.01	2.41	2.18	−40.86	−17.25	23.61
Switzerland	0.37	0.92	0.58	−54.47	−20.71	33.76
Thailand	3.23	3.05	3.37	17.84	−14.69	−32.53
1994						
Argentina	0.00	0.45	0.47	−45.11	−47.30	−2.20
Australia	0.35	0.07	−0.09	28.30	44.18	15.88
Austria	2.48	2.69	2.47	−20.97	1.96	22.94
Britain	−0.38	−0.24	−0.39	−13.94	0.81	14.75
Canada	0.33	0.22	0.04	11.42	28.47	17.05

Table A3.1   Continued

Country	Logarithmic			Logarithmic differences × 100		
	Actual exchange rate (ER) (1)	Big Mac Index (BMI) (2)	No-Frills Index (NFI) (3)	Actual ER-BMI (4) = (1) − (2)	Actual ER-NFI (5) = (1) − (3)	BMI-NFI (6) = (2) − (3)
Chile	6.03	6.02	6.23	0.48	−20.38	−20.87
China	2.16	1.36	2.10	79.98	6.16	−73.82
Denmark	1.90	2.42	2.16	−51.53	−25.52	26.01
France	1.76	2.08	1.87	−32.14	−10.89	21.25
Germany	0.54	0.69	0.49	−15.67	5.03	20.69
Greece	5.53	5.60	5.60	−7.30	−7.75	−0.45
Holland	0.65	0.86	0.66	−21.58	−1.66	19.92
Hungary	4.63	4.30	4.49	33.77	14.93	−18.85
Italy	7.40	7.59	7.43	−18.68	−2.82	15.86
Japan	4.64	5.14	4.80	−49.14	−15.88	33.26
Malaysia	0.99	0.49	0.72	49.48	26.79	−22.70
Mexico	1.21	1.26	1.45	−4.65	−23.76	−19.11
Poland	10.02	9.51	9.82	50.95	19.48	−31.47
Portugal	5.16	5.25	5.28	−9.32	−12.27	−2.95
Russia	7.48	7.14	7.47	34.19	1.64	−32.54
Singapore	0.45	0.26	0.04	18.87	41.20	22.33
South Korea	6.70	6.91	6.92	−21.07	−22.53	−1.46
Spain	4.93	5.01	4.94	−8.34	−1.62	6.72
Sweden	2.08	2.41	2.20	−33.13	−12.01	21.12
Switzerland	0.36	0.91	0.58	−54.36	−21.88	32.48
Thailand	3.23	3.04	3.36	19.25	−12.58	−31.83
Mean				−10.12	0.00	10.12
Standard error of mean				2.81	2.26	1.59
t-statistic				−3.61	0.00	6.38

Notes

1. Froot and Rogoff (1995) and Officer (1982) provide comprehensive reviews of the literature.
2. See, for instance, Balassa (1964), Froot and Rogoff (1995) and Keynes (1930).
3. *Look Japan*, June 1994, p. 38.
4. Pakko and Pollard (1996) provide an independent analysis of Big Mac PPP. In that paper, the authors investigate the performance of

absolute and relative Big Mac PPP, and they also provide a discussion on why PPP fails.

5. See, for example, Frenkel (1981), Manzur (1990) and Officer (1976).
6. According to Cumby (1996), deviations from Big Mac PPP are useful for forecasting exchange rates. After accounting for currency-specific constants, a 10 per cent undervaluation in one year, according to the Big Mac Index, is associated with a 3.5 per cent appreciation over the following year.
7. Engel and Rogers (1996) look at the significance of physical distance for PPP. They show that 'crossing the border' is equivalent to adding 7182 miles between two cities in the same country.
8. Frankel and Rose (1996), Hakkio (1984) and Oh (1996) show that the higher variability in cross-sectional data relative to time-series data allows for more precise parameter estimates in tests of PPP. Similarly, Cumby (1996) demonstrates that a larger cross-section yields enough power to detect substantial mean-reversion in his tests of Big Mac PPP. He finds little persistence in deviations from Big Mac PPP, with only 30 per cent of deviations persisting into the following year.
9. Hakkio (1984) and Frankel and Rose (1996) show that higher variability in cross-sectional data relative to time-series data allows for more precise parameter estimates.
10. See Blundell-Wignall *et al.* (1993), Edison and Pauls (1993) and Froot and Rogoff (1995). Note that as our data observations are both across countries and over time, non-stationarity may not be such a problem as compared with the situation with pure time-series data.
11. For instance, Harrod (1939, p. 71) argues that the costs of transportation of commodities across borders, and the effects of tariffs on those commodities, would result in the divergence of purchasing power between two economies within the limits imposed by these costs.
12. In Japan, for instance, the cost of imported beef (which accounts for nearly 80 per cent of the ingredients in a Big Mac) includes a 50 per cent tariff (*Look Japan*, June 1994, p. 38).
13. See Ghosh and Wolf (1994).
14. Cumby (1996) finds that relative local currency prices appear to adjust to reduce deviations from Big Mac PPP.
15. To estimate equation (3.17), we use the data on r calculated in our discussion on the valuation of currencies (p. 55) and GDP data obtained from the *International Financial Statistics* of the International Monetary Fund.
16. See Appendix 3.1 for the derivation of the NFI.

References

Balassa, B. (1964) 'The Purchasing-Power Parity Doctrine: A Reappraisal', *Journal of Political Economy*, vol. 72, pp. 584–96.

Blundell-Wignall, A., J. Fahrer and A. Heath (1993) 'Major Influences on the Australian Dollar Exchange Rate', *The Exchange Rate, International Trade and the Balance of Payments*, Proceedings of a Conference held at the H.C. Coombs Centre for Financial Studies, Kirribilli.

Clements, K. W. and J. A. Frenkel (1980) 'Exchange Rates, Money, and Relative Prices: The Dollar-Pound in the 1920s', *Journal of International Economics*, vol. 10, pp. 249–62.

Clements, K. W. and M. Semudram (1983) 'An International Comparison of the Price of Nontraded Goods', *Weltwirtschaftliches Archiv*, vol. 119, pp. 356–63.

Cumby, R. (1996) 'Forecasting Exchange Rates on the Hamburger Standard: What You See is What You Get with McParity', NBER Working Paper Series, no. 5675, National Bureau of Economic Research, Cambridge, Massachusetts.

Edison, H. J. and B. D. Pauls (1993) 'A Re-assessment of the Relationship between Real Exchange Rates and Real Interest Rates: 1974–90', *Journal of Monetary Economics*, vol. 31, pp. 165–87.

Engel, C. and J. H. Rogers (1996) 'How Wide is the Border?', *American Economic Review*, vol. 86, pp. 1112–25.

Frankel, J. A. and A. Rose (1996) 'A Panel Project on Purchasing Power Parity: Mean Reversion within and between Countries', *Journal of International Economics*, vol. 40, pp. 209–24.

Frankel, J. A. and S. J. Wei (1993) 'Is there a Currency Bloc in the Pacific?', in *Exchange Rates, International Trade and the Balance of Payments*, ed. Adrian Blundert Wignall, pp. 275–308. Sydney: Reserve Bank of Australia.

Frankel, J. A. and S. J. Wei (1995) 'Is a Yen Bloc Emerging?', in *Economic Cooperation and Challenges in the Pacific*, ed. R. Rich, pp. 145–75. Washington, DC: Korea Economic Institute of America.

Frenkel, J. A. (1981) 'The Collapse of Purchasing Power Parities During the 1970s', *European Economic Review*, vol. 16, pp. 145–65.

Froot, K. A. and K. Rogoff (1995) 'Perspectives on PPP and Long-Run Real Exchange Rates', in *Handbook of International Economics*, eds G. Grossman and K. Rogoff, vol. 3, pp. 1647–88. Amsterdam: North-Holland.

Ghosh, A. R. and H. C. Wolf (1994) 'Pricing in International Markets: Lessons from *The Economist*', NBER Working Paper Series, no. 4806, National Bureau of Economic Research, Cambridge, Massachusetts.

Hakkio, C. S. (1984) 'A Re-Examination of Purchasing Power Parity: A Multi-Country and Multi-Period Study,' *Journal of International Economics*, vol. 17, pp. 265–77.

Harrod, R. F. (1939) *International Economics*. Cambridge: Nisbet & Co.

Keynes, J. M. (1930), *A Treatise on Money*, vol. 1. London: Palgrave Macmillan.

Look Japan, vol. 40, no. 459. Tokyo: Look Japan Ltd.

Manzur, M. (1990), 'An International Comparison of Prices and Exchange Rates: A New Test of Purchasing Power Parity', *Journal of International Money and Finance*, vol. 9, pp. 75–91.

Officer, L. H. (1976) 'The Purchasing-Power-Parity Theory of Exchange Rates: A Review Article', *IMF Staff Papers*, no. 23, pp. 1–60.

Officer, L. H. (1982) *Purchasing Power Parity and Exchange Rates: Theory, Evidence and Relevance.* Connecticut: JAI Press.

Oh, K. Y. (1996) 'Purchasing Power Parity and Unit Root Tests Using Panel Data', *Journal of International Money and Finance*, vol. 15, pp. 405–18.

Pakko, M. R. and P. S. Pollard (1996) 'For Here or To Go? Purchasing Power Parity and the Big Mac', *Federal Reserve Bank of St. Louis Review*, vol. 78, pp. 3–21.

The Economist, various issues.

4

'Burgernomics' and the ASEAN Currency Crisis*

The decimation of ASEAN currency markets in 1997 shows why Big Macs should be a staple item in every economist's diet ...

Introduction

The theory of purchasing power parity (PPP) states that the rate of exchange between two currencies is determined by the price levels in the two economies. In other words, the prices of a basket of similar goods and services in two countries *should be equal* when converted to a common currency. To the extent that the prices are not equalized, the exchange rate is said to be misaligned. *The Economist* (26 August 1995, p. 70) provides a good analogy on exchange rate misalignments:

> Suppose a man climbs five feet up a sea wall, then climbs down 12 feet. Whether he drowns or not depends upon how high above sea-level he was when he started. The same problem arises in deciding whether currencies are under- or over-valued.

In recent years, research into the accuracy of the Big Mac Index as a measure of PPP between countries has generally concluded that the index performs just as well as, if not better than, most indices used in tests of PPP.[1] In fact, Ong (1997) boldly asserts that the Big Mac Index is 'extraordinarily accurate' in tracking exchange rates. However, news in February 1997 that McDonald's was about to reduce drastically the

---

* Published in the *Journal of the Australian Society of Security Analysts*, Autumn 1998, pp. 15–16.

US price of its Big Mac by 65 per cent to about US$0.85, caused *The Economist* magazine and fans of burgernomics to stew over the possibility that the infamous hamburger standard would be 'reduced to ashes' by this new development.

The *Economist's* Big Mac Index, published on 12 April 1997, suggested at the time that the currencies of member countries of the Association of South-East Asian Nations (ASEAN) were generally undervalued against the US dollar. The Malaysian ringgit, Singaporean dollar and Thai baht were undervalued by about 45, 15 and 30 per cent, respectively.[2] Meanwhile, the Indonesian rupiah was undervalued by 24 per cent and the Philippine peso by 39 per cent.[3] This is in line with earlier findings that ASEAN currencies have consistently been undervalued against the US dollar over the last decade.[4] The proposed devaluation of the US Big Mac price would have indeed landed the Index in hot soup, as it would have instantly presented these developing country currencies as being substantially and uncharacteristically overvalued by approximately 60 to 90 per cent (see Figure 4.1).[5] At that point, only a major devaluation of these currencies could redeem the hamburger standard.

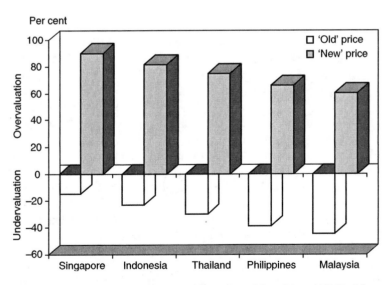

Figure 4.1   Valuation of currencies based on the 'old' and 'new' US Big Mac prices.

Currencies in crisis

Events in ASEAN currency markets in the weeks leading up to September 1997 left the burger-sceptics choking on humble pie and further boosted the stock of burgernomics in the financial markets. Many reasons and recriminations have since been offered for the depreciation of these currencies, the unexpectedness and viciousness with which it happened: speculative attacks led by the international financier, George Soros; excessive foreign debt levels from using foreign funds to finance high levels of economic expansion; increasingly unsustainable current account deficits caused by surging imports; high and constantly-rising capital inflows. In hindsight, this was a Molotov cocktail just waiting to explode. However, as any avid burgerette knows, these currencies were already ripe for the picking when the announcement of the US Big Mac price cut was made.

The recent experience with the ASEAN currencies bears testimony to the versatility of the Big Mac Index as a pricing model for foreign exchange. The index suggested that the currencies needed to fall dramatically to restore parity, and tumble they did. Up to 3 September 1997, the baht had plunged 26 per cent against the US dollar since April, the ringgit had depreciated 12 per cent, while the peso and the rupiah had fallen 14 and 18 per cent, respectively. Found guilty by association, the Singaporean dollar lost 5 per cent. The domino-effects of these devaluations – higher interest payments on foreign debt, higher interest costs of financing investments in real assets and the impending economic slowdown, higher import prices and subsequent inflation – was a recipe for further problems. Based on the Big Mac Index, further currency devaluations were imminent. At that stage, only the very brave would have bet against these currencies being sliced up further in the coming months.[6] By the end of January 1998, the rupiah had declined by 159 per cent from its April 1997 value, the baht and the ringgit were almost at parity, having lost 72 and 56 per cent respectively against the US dollar, and the peso was down 47 per cent. Caught up in the region's turmoil despite its strong economic fundamentals, Singapore's dollar had fallen 18 per cent over that period.

If the sceptics need further convincing, one should point out that in the years leading to the Mexican peso getting its just desserts in 1995, the Big Mac Index had indicated the peso to be overvalued. The financial community should pay closer attention the next time Mr Soros orders a Big Mac to go.

Notes

1. See Click (1996), Cumby (1996), Ong (1997), and Pakko and Pollard (1996).
2. The over- or undervaluation of a currency relative to the US dollar is calculated as $r_{ct} \equiv \log[(P_{ct}/P_t^*)/S_{ct}] = \log(P_{ct}/P_t^*) - \log S_{ct}$, where P_{ct} is the domestic currency price of a Big Mac in country c in year t; P_t^* is the price in US dollars of a Big Mac in the US; and S_{ct} is the spot exchange rate, defined as the domestic currency cost of US\$1. Accordingly, P_{ct}/P_t^* is the Big Mac PPP. A currency is said to be overvalued if r_{ct} is greater than zero, undervalued if r_{ct} is less than zero and at parity if r_{ct} equals zero. The percentage deviation from parity is approximately $r_{ct} \times 100$.
3. I am grateful to Grace Dharmawan and Princeton Tan for providing the Big Mac prices for Indonesia and the Philippines, respectively. The corresponding exchange rates are obtained from *The Economist*.
4. Ong (1997) shows that the Malaysian ringgit, Singaporean dollar and Thai baht have, on average, been respectively undervalued by approximately 53, 26 and 19 per cent against the US dollar over the 1986 to 1994 period.
5. Ong (1997) demonstrates that the undervaluation of developing economy currencies can be attributed largely to the productivity bias hypothesis or the 'Balassa–Samuelson' effect. This hypothesis states that since richer countries have a greater productivity advantage in traded goods relative to non-traded goods, the relative price of non-traded goods will be higher in those countries. The currencies of richer countries will thus appear overvalued in PPP terms, because non-traded goods enter into the calculation of PPP but not the exchange rate.
6. Although it is highly unlikely that the Singaporean dollar will devalue by another 85 per cent to restore Big Mac PPP, further devaluations are not unlikely given its position as Malaysia's second-largest trade and investment partner.

References

Balassa, B. (1964) 'The Purchasing-Power Parity Doctrine: A Reappraisal', *Journal of Political Economy*, vol. 72, pp. 584–96.

Click, R. W. (1996) 'Contrarian MacParity', *Economics Letters*, vol. 53, pp. 209–12.

Cumby, R. (1996) 'Forecasting Exchange Rates on the Hamburger Standard: What You See is What You Get with McParity', NBER Working Paper Series, no. 5675, National Bureau of Economic Research, Cambridge, Massachusetts.

Ong, L. L. (1997) 'Burgernomics: The Economics of the Big Mac Standard', *Journal of International Money and Finance*, vol. 16, pp. 865–78.

Pakko, M. R. and P. S. Pollard (1996) 'For Here or To Go? Purchasing Power Parity and the Big Mac', *Federal Reserve Bank of St. Louis Review*, vol. 78, pp. 3–21.

Samuelson, P. A. (1964) 'Theoretical Notes on Trade Problems', *Review of Economics and Statistics*, vol. 46, pp. 145–54.

The Economist, 26 August 1995; 12 April 1997.

5

Big Macs and Wages To Go, Please: Comparing the Purchasing Power of Earnings Around the World*

> The diversity across countries in measured per capita income levels is literally too great to be believed. Compared to the 1980 average for what the World Bank calls the 'industrialized market economies' ... of US$10,000, India's per capita income is $240, Haiti's is $270, and so on for the rest of the very poorest countries. This is a difference of 40 in living standards! These latter figures are too low to sustain life in, say, England or the United States, so they cannot be taken at face value.
>
> (Robert E. Lucas Jr, 1988, pp. 3–4)

The relocating employee's main concern is that the current standard of living can be maintained or improved in the destination country. This means that their purchasing power cannot fall. However, comparing home- and destination-country prices based on the existing exchange rate would be inappropriate since exchange rates only reflect purchasing power parity (PPP) in the long term. Thus, an index for *real* wages and expenses should be created whereby these prices are converted into *purchasing power equivalents* for each country. Using an index based on the 'perfect universal commodity', the Big Mac hamburger, as a price deflator, the real wages and major relocation expenses for US employees in some of the biggest commercial cities around the world are considered in this chapter.

---

* Published in the *Australian Journal of Labour Economics*, vol. 2, pp. 53–68 (1998).

A model is subsequently developed whereby real wages can be approximated based on the market status and geographic location of the destination country. The results indicate that US employees would generally be worse off moving overseas if they are to be paid destination-country wages to take up similar positions; moreover, major expenditure items such as accommodation and cars are also extremely expensive in certain foreign cities. These findings can be used by multinational companies (MNCs), their employees, as well as economic migrants to define equitable and attractive salary packages.

Introduction

In an increasingly advanced and highly integrated world economy, natural resources, capital availability (both physical and financial) and labour skills have lost much of their former exclusivity. Businesses now operate in an era of artificial materials and genetic engineering, improving technological ability and fewer capital restrictions, cross-border education programmes and increasing labour mobility.[1] The expansion of trade in goods and services has resulted in markets for skilled workers in MNCs and skilled professionals (economic migrants) in search of economic opportunities abroad.[2] While MNCs often try to reduce the implicit costs of relocation by recruiting their employees directly in foreign countries, problems arise when such expertise is unavailable in the host country and must be 'sent' from the home country (Chelminski and Chong, 1993).[3]

Occasionally, MNC employees are prepared to accept a lower standard of living and the tax consequences of working overseas in exchange for the experience.[4] At other times, employees gain windfalls from currency fluctuations or benefit from paying little tax.[5] From the point of view of the company, the wages of expatriate employees should ensure that while sufficient incentives are provided to relocate, employees should not gain excessively from going overseas to work as this may result in a disincentive to return home (Delia-Loyle, 1992).

According to Bennett (1996), the 'destination approach' adopted by MNCs in recent years has seen global expatriate pay move away from home-country standards towards a peer-based pay system. This means that local wage levels have become a major consideration for relocating employees. The difficulty for all parties arises when trying to determine what constitutes an attractive salary package since the existence of wage and purchasing power differentials between the home and foreign countries could have significant bearing on living standards. For the economic migrant, it is important to ensure that living standards can at least be maintained and preferably improved. Moreover, Lewis (1997) observes that while temporary residents are more concerned about economic rewards, economic migrants are additionally concerned about their lifestyle in the destination country.

Economic literature has shown that wages are positively related to productivity. Oulton (1994), for instance, argues that both labour costs and labour productivity must be taken into account when assessing a country's competitiveness, since high wages are usually accompanied by high productivity and vice versa.[6] Balassa's (1964) productivity bias hypothesis suggests that wages are relatively higher in richer countries as a result of higher productivity. This is demonstrated by Clements and Semudram (1983) who find that the costs of services increase with increasing gross domestic product (GDP). Does this mean, then, that wages in poorer countries are unattractive? Not necessarily, since it is the *purchasing power* of these wages that is most important.

The main aim of this chapter is to consider several important issues faced by relocating employees *who are paid foreign-country wages*, as well as economic migrants. For instance, (1) would receiving foreign-country wages be sufficient incentive for relocation? (2) what is the effect of taxes on wages across countries? (3) what is the effect of purchasing power differentials on living standards? (4) do the geographic location and market status of the destination country matter? To answer these questions, the average real wages (gross and net) for 27 major commercial cities around the world is considered from the viewpoint of the US MNC employee/economic migrant (the relocating employee). In other words, the nominal wage in each country is converted to US *purchasing power equivalents* using a relative price index. A standardized price index is used in place of the conventional exchange rate for more accurate comparisons because it has been well-documented that purchasing power differentials between countries are only reflected in exchange rates in the long-run.[7] The use of exchange rates for short-term comparisons would only be appropriate if the employee could somehow contrive to use the income earned in the foreign country to purchase goods and services in the home country on a daily basis.[8]

The wages data for 27 cities for 1988, 1991 and 1994 are obtained from the Union Bank of Switzerland, which publishes the information on a triennial basis.[9] The wages are then deflated to US purchasing power equivalents using *The Economist*'s Big Mac Index to give a more useful comparison of costs of living between countries. First introduced in 1986 as a tongue-in-cheek look at the PPP concept, the Big Mac is made to the same recipe in over 80 countries around the world. It is widely regarded as the 'perfect universal commodity' in that it represents a standard basket of goods and services across countries; moreover, it is easily obtainable for comparison purposes and intuitively appealing.[10]

Overall, real wages are found to be positively related to real GDP per capita; this means that US employees are generally worse off if they are paid destination-country wages. The results also show that taxes are significantly different across countries and must be taken into account. Furthermore, the market status and geographic location of the destination country are also very important. As a result, a general wage-pricing model is developed whereby real wages can be calculated depending on whether the destination country is an emerging or developed economy, as well as according to its geographic location.

In the next section, both the net and gross real wages across countries are compared against the US; the relationship between real wages and GDP is also tested. We then focus on developing a model which can be used to approximate real wages in different markets (developed versus emerging markets) as well as the different regions around the world. As an extension, the real costs of accommodation and transportation are then compared to determine which major relocation expenses could/should be salary-packaged. Here, comparisons are made between 'executive' and 'local' housing areas, while the different transportation alternatives considered are public transportation, taxi and maintaining a car.

On paycheques and purchasing power

Consider the situation where a US employee relocates to a foreign city and is paid in local wages. A very important concern would be whether the employee's purchasing power, and thus standard of living, can be maintained overseas. To give an example: if a Big Mac costs US$2.30 in the US and SFr5.70 in Switzerland, then the relocating employee would require a wage of SFr5.70 in Switzerland for every US$2.30 earned in New York in order to purchase a similar lifestyle. To the extent that this is not true, the employee is said to have less or greater purchasing power in the foreign city.[11]

In order to determine if the *real* wages in a foreign city are lower or greater than New York, the following is calculated:

$$r \equiv \log\left(\frac{P/s}{P^\star}\right) \equiv \log\frac{P/(P_{BM}/P_{BM}^\star)}{P^\star} \equiv \log\frac{(P/P^\star)}{(P_{BM}/P_{BM}^\star)} \tag{5.1}$$

where P is the foreign currency wage in the foreign city; $P^\star$ is the US dollar wage in New York; and $s = P_{BM}/P_{BM}^\star$ is the Big Mac PPP cost of foreign currency per US dollar. That is, is the ratio of the local cost of a Big Mac in the country in question to the US$ cost in the US. Thus, r is equal to zero if $P/P^\star = P_{BM}/P_{BM}^\star$; local wages are said to have greater purchasing power than the US if r is greater than zero; and less purchasing power if r is less than zero. The percentage foreign wage differential from the New York wage is approximately $r \times 100$.

Table 5.1 gives the percentage real wage differentials (gross and net) relative to the US, averaged over the 1988 to 1994 period. Assuming that US employees receive destination-country wages for a similar position, the purchasing power of their gross local wages would have been lower than in New York had they relocated to any major city in the world other than Copenhagen or Toronto. However, the differentials between New York and local real wages change once taxes and social security contributions are deducted as a result of differing tax rates between countries. For instance, real *gross* wages are 16 per cent *higher* in Copenhagen than in New York, but real *net* wages there are 19 per cent *lower*; in Toronto, real gross wages are 4 per cent higher, while real net wages are even higher, by 7 per cent.

The high tax rates and social security contributions in Europe mean that the purchasing power of net wages is lower in Europe after accounting for taxes.[12] Although taxes are more favourable in the emerging Latin American and Asian economies, real net wages in these countries are also lower than in the US. Thus, it is important to consider the purchasing power of *net* wages rather than their gross amounts.

Table 5.1 Real wage differentials relative to the US, 1988–94 averages (in percentages)

City	Wages	
	Gross	Net
Developed markets		
Amsterdam	−28	−43
Brussels	−26	−44
Copenhagen	16	−19
Dublin	−33	−33
Frankfurt	−3	−16
London	−32	−45
Madrid	−59	−66
Milan	−39	−51
Paris	−56	−65
Stockholm	−47	−74
Vienna	−40	−48
Zurich	−25	−26
Sydney	−7	−3
Tokyo	−14	−15
Toronto	**4**	**7**
Emerging markets		
Athens	−106	−105
Lisbon	−126	−127
Budapest	−192	−205
Prague	−213	−214
Buenos Aires	−150	−145
Mexico City	−172	−165
São Paulo	−148	−146
Hong Kong	−53	−18
Seoul	−88	−103
Taipei	−70	−57
Bangkok	−185	−170
Singapore	−100	−88

Notes
1 Net wages are after deducting taxes and social security contributions.
2 Figures in bold indicate instances where real wages are higher relative to the US.
3 Athens and Lisbon are classified as 'emerging markets' in this instance due to their very low real wage levels.

Source: *Prices and Earnings Around the Globe*, Union Bank of Switzerland, 1988/91/94.

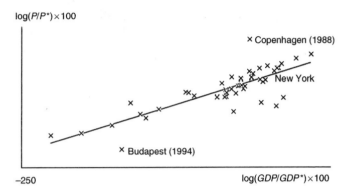

Figure 5.1   Relative real net wages and real GDP per capita, 1988–94

Further observation of Table 5.1 suggests that real wages in the emerging markets are generally much lower than their developed-market counterparts. These observations are subsequently formalized by testing the relationship between real net wages and real GDP per capita across countries:

$$\log\left(\frac{p}{P^*}\right) = \alpha + \beta \log\left(\frac{GDP}{GDP^*}\right) \qquad (5.2)$$

where $p = P/s$ is the real wage in the foreign country. In other words, the real wages in the foreign city relative to New York are compared against the relative real wealth (GDP per capita) between the two countries.

The regression (5.2) results are presented in Figure 5.1. The adjusted R^2 of 65 per cent, with an estimated elasticity coefficient ($\hat{\beta}$) of 0.79, suggests a strong positive relationship between real wages and GDP per capita.[13] The general conclusion is that real net wages are lower in the poorer emerging markets compared to the developed economies as a result of productivity differentials. This is consistent with existing empirical evidence discussed earlier.

Who gets what where?

The findings in the previous section suggest that the pricing of labour can be modelled based on the status of the economy, as well as its

geographic location. Subsequently, each city in the sample is catego-
rized as either (1) emerging market or (2) developed market; *and* (1)
North America, (2) Central and South America, (3) Western and
Central Europe, (4) Eastern Europe, or (5) Asia-Oceania.

The following dummy-variable regression based on those
categories is then implemented:

$$r = \gamma + a \cdot EM + b \cdot CSA + c \cdot WCE + d \cdot EE + e \cdot AO \qquad (5.3)$$

where the intercept *g* represents the joint-variable for North America
and developed markets; *EM* represents the dummy variable for
emerging markets; *CSA* represents Central and South America; *WCE*
represents Western and Central Europe; *EE* represents Eastern
Europe; and *AO* represents Asia-Oceania. The results from regression
(5.3) are given in Table 5.2.

The results indicate that a significant relationship exists between
real (net) wages and whether the city is situated in an emerging or
developed economy. In addition, the region in which the city is
located also appears to play a significant role in defining the real wages
relative to New York (see Figure 5.2).[14] The exception is Asia-Oceania,
where the dummy variable for emerging markets appears to capture
most of the relative wage information related to these markets.

Using the model, it is clear that Toronto, which is situated in a
developed economy in North America, pays wages with approximately 7 per cent higher purchasing power than New York, on average. Meanwhile, real net wages in emerging Eastern European
markets are approximately (7–87–125) 205 per cent below New York;
wages in developed markets in Western and Central Europe are

Table 5.2 Regression results: relative real net wages, market status and
geographic location, 1988–94 (standard errors in parentheses)

Adjusted R^2		0.65	
Standard error of regression		30.79	
Intercept coefficient	$\hat{\gamma}$	6.96	(17.77)
Dummy variable coefficients			
Emerging markets (*EM*)	$\hat{a}$	−87.29	(14.35)
Central and South America (*CSA*)	$\hat{b}$	−74.47	(31.56)
Western and Central Europe (*WCE*)	$\hat{c}$	−49.70	(18.59)
Eastern Europe (*EE*)	$\hat{d}$	−124.99	(38.34)
Asia-Oceania (*AO*)	$\hat{e}$	−21.52	(21.53)

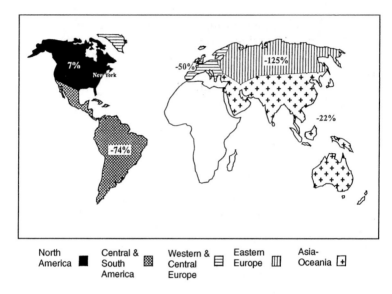

North
America ■

Central &
South ▨
America

Western &
Central ☰
Europe

Eastern
Europe ▥

Asia-
Oceania ⊞

Figure 5.2   Relative real wages by region: 1988–94 averages

approximately (7–49) 42 per cent lower. Of the Asia-Oceania cities, the purchasing power of net wages in Sydney and Tokyo is not significantly different from New York.

Further extensions: accommodation and transportation

In this section, the major costs normally associated with relocation, namely accommodation and transportation, are considered. For the MNC employee, these items could be salary-packaged, while economic migrants should take them into account when considering job opportunities overseas as they could have a significant bearing on their lifestyle. Using the equation (5.1) formula, P and P^* are redefined as the price of accommodation/transportation in the foreign city and New York, respectively. The real costs of these items relative to New York are presented in Table 5.3.

Clearly, accommodation in most cities is relatively cheaper in real terms compared to New York, regardless of whether 'executive' apartments or 'local' accommodation is selected. This is not true in

Table 5.3 Real cost of living differentials relative to the US, 1988–94 averages (in percentages)

City	Accommodation		Transportation costs			
	Executive apartment	Local average	Car price	Car maintenance	Public transport	Taxi
Developed markets						
Amsterdam	−106	−124	**14**	**40**	**2**	**4**
Brussels	−127	−94	**6**	−17	−17	−10
Copenhagen	−149	−108	**59**	**58**	**57**	**10**
Dublin	−125	−110	**64**	**32**	**28**	**10**
Frankfurt	−100	−70	**25**	**37**	**7**	**3**
London	−65	−34	**36**	**23**	**48**	**6**
Madrid	−98	−79	**21**	−45	−25	−65
Milan	−105	−99	**12**	**8**	−68	**12**
Paris	−107	−86	**4**	−93	−51	−31
Stockholm	−160	−143	**9**	−43	**38**	−17
Vienna	−113	−104	**30**	**64**	**8**	**24**
Zurich	−116	−78	−8	**33**	**3**	**26**
Sydney	−77	−64	**57**	**27**	**59**	−2
Tokyo	**54**	−29	**14**	**77**	−13	**13**
Toronto	−77	−17	**15**	−21	**17**	**14**
Emerging markets						
Athens	−128	−84	**78**	−9	−151	−118
Lisbon	−123	−40	**62**	−93	−92	−62
Budapest	−173	−76	**75**	−44	−131	−35
Prague	−114	−284	−12	N/A	−152	−57
Buenos Aires	−186	−124	−5	**113**	−100	−51
Mexico City	−57	−106	**4**	**77**	−239	−95
São Paulo	−37	−30	**62**	**141**	−99	−41
Hong Kong	**129**	**67**	**128**	**154**	**20**	−5
Seoul	−103	−13	−32	−198	−107	−21
Taipei	−83	−11	**29**	**29**	−114	−64
Bangkok	−21	−87	**128**	−5	−105	−36
Singapore	−7	**33**	**175**	**159**	−44	−78

Notes
1 Executive apartments are in the medium price range, 4-bedroom, fully-furnished and situated in or near the city centre.
2 Car price is that of a popular medium-sized, 4-door standard model. Car maintenance costs include road taxes, annual registration fee and average service labour costs. Petrol costs are not included.
3 Price of public transport and taxi include a 20 km round-trip per day for 300 days.
4 Figures in bold indicate instances where real costs are higher relative to the US.

Source: Prices and Earnings Around the Globe, Union Bank of Switzerland, 1988/91/94.

Hong Kong, where executive apartments are 129 per cent more expensive and average local housing is 67 per cent more expensive than their New York equivalents. Executive apartments are also more expensive in Tokyo, on average. Car prices and their maintenance costs in New York are amongst the cheapest in the world; only in Seoul are cars cheaper and maintenance costs lower. The price of cars is exorbitant in Bangkok, Hong Kong and Singapore. However, public transportation and taxi fares are much cheaper overseas, with the exception of a handful of Western European cities.

Table 5.4 shows the average purchasing power (in US dollars) available to the expatriate employee after taking into account taxes, accommodation and transportation in cities around the world. Column 1 gives the net wage levels in PPP dollars, relative to a hypothetical real net wage of US$80000 in New York. These figures are based on the real net wage differentials given in Table 5.1. As an example, the average net wage in Prague during this period would have purchased a lifestyle-equivalent of US$9378 in New York, compared to purchasing power of US$80000 earned in New York itself. Similarly, the purchasing power of net wages in other emerging economies such as Hungary, Mexico and Thailand is very low – less than the equivalent of US$20000 in New York. On the other hand, the average net wage in Toronto would have purchased a lifestyle equivalent to that of US$85764 in New York.

The real costs of accommodation and transportation are subsequently deducted from the net wages in column 1 – assuming that these costs are met by the US employee who is earning foreign wages – to determine the purchasing power available for other living expenses. When comparing executive-type accommodation (columns 3 to 5), the employee would be relatively better off in Brussels, Copenhagen, Dublin, Frankfurt, Sydney, Toronto and Zurich, regardless of the type of transportation expenditure. Moreover, the increase in purchasing power also means that cars, albeit more expensive than in New York, are affordable in these cities. Not surprisingly, the prices of cars in Bangkok, Hong Kong and Singapore are extremely expensive given the respective governments' drive to reduce traffic congestion. Executive-style housing would be totally unaffordable in Bangkok, Hong Kong, Mexico City, Prague, São Paulo and Singapore. Meanwhile, employees who live in local rental areas would be relatively better-off in Sydney and Toronto compared to New York (columns 6 to 8).

Table 5.4 Real net wages after taxes, accommodation and transportation costs, 1988–94 averages (in US PPP dollars)

City	Net wages (1)	Car price (2)	Net wages after accommodation and transportation costs less					
			'Executive' apartment rental less			'Local' apartment rental less		
			Car maintenance (3)	Public transport (4)	Taxi (5)	Car maintenance (6)	Public transport (7)	Taxi (8)
New York	80 000	11 233	36 172	35 720	27 980	64 292	63 840	56 100
Developed markets								
Amsterdam	51 848	12 915	36 354	36 000	27 950	47 027	46 673	38 623
Brussels	51 643	11 947	39 167	38 783	31 730	45 407	45 023	37 970
Copenhagen	65 882	20 230	55 672	54 882	46 775	60 242	59 452	51 346
Dublin	57 451	21 265	44 687	44 102	35 666	51 991	51 406	42 970
Frankfurt	67 898	14 457	51 490	51 092	43 170	59 854	59 456	51 534
London	50 938	16 059	27 880	27 065	19 190	39 592	38 778	30 903
Madrid	41 189	13 834	24 675	24 292	20 441	34 012	33 629	29 778
Milan	48 061	12 604	32 609	32 511	23 395	42 090	41 992	32 876
Paris	41 756	11 706	26 654	26 334	20 582	35 137	34 818	29 066
Stockholm	38 042	12 242	29 134	28 292	22 207	34 190	33 348	27 263
Vienna	49 263	15 173	34 810	34 507	24 495	43 378	43 074	33 063
Zurich	61 834	10 414	47 887	47 503	37 241	54 424	54 040	43 777
Sydney	77 464	19 954	56 961	56 037	48 998	68 991	68 067	61 028
Tokyo	68 747	12 887	-6505	-6608	-15 634	56 699	56 597	47 570
Toronto	85 764	13 032	65 440	64 823	55 905	72 528	71 910	62 992
Emerging markets								
Athens	28 056	24 407	15 762	15 821	13 393	21 134	21 193	18 765
Lisbon	22 469	20 859	9591	9410	5165	11 976	11 795	7550
Budapest	10 266	23 847	2383	2347	-3416	2864	2828	-2935

Table 5.4 Continued

| City | Net wages (1) | Car price (2) | Net wages after accommodation and transportation costs less | | | | | |
| | | | 'Executive' apartment rental less | | | 'Local' apartment rental less | | |
			Car maintenance (3)	Public transport (4)	Taxi (5)	Car maintenance (6)	Public transport (7)	Taxi (8)
Prague	9378	**9964**	N/A	−4653	−9245	N/A	8321	3729
Buenos Aires	18 781	10 684	11 318	11 772	6952	13 615	14 069	9249
Mexico City	15 413	11 639	−9850	−9417	−12 607	9538	9971	6782
São Paulo	18 591	20 884	−12 382	−11 696	−17 036	6241	6927	1587
Hong Kong	66 947	40 588	−91 930	−91 703	−98 917	35 737	35 964	28 749
Seoul	28 508	**8185**	12 863	12 660	6092	14 944	14 741	8173
Taipei	45 123	15 006	25 717	25 805	21 599	30 977	31 065	26 859
Bangkok	14 582	40 314	−21 129	−21 149	−26 796	7906	7886	2240
Singapore	33 317	64 967	−8457	−7770	−11 193	10 707	11 395	7972

Note: Figures in bold indicate instances where the US MNC employee is better off, in PPP terms, in the foreign country.

Source: Table 5.1, based on hypothetical net wages of US$80 000 in New York and actual costs published in *Prices and Earnings Around the Globe*, Union Bank of Switzerland, 1988/91/94.

Conclusion

It is only natural that both relocating MNC employees, who are increasingly earning destination-country wages, and economic migrants would want to be able to maintain or improve their existing standard of living in the foreign country. In order to do so, however, issues such as differentials in wage levels, taxes and purchasing power are foremost considerations. Thus, a major step towards resolving this conflict is to consider the *real* wages paid to employees; that is, the purchasing power of wages earned.

Firstly, the findings here suggest that real wage differences should be considered net of tax, given the obvious tax differentials between countries. Secondly, it appears that net wages in major commercial cities around the world generally have less purchasing power than in New York; that is, standards of living are lower elsewhere. This suggests that US employees would generally be worse off moving to a similar job in a foreign country for local wages, without additional incentives being provided. There also appears to be a significant relationship between real net wages and GDP, and between real net wages and geographic location. Thus, a wage-pricing model has been developed which can be used by relocating employees to determine the real wages for a foreign city, based on whether it is located in an emerging or developed market, and whether it is situated in South America, Eastern Europe, and so on.

The study is subsequently extended to consider major relocation expenses. Specifically, the destination country's costs of accommodation and transportation in US purchasing power equivalents are considered. The results suggest that executive accommodation could be provided as an added incentive for US MNC employees relocating to cities such as Bangkok, Hong Kong, São Paulo and Singapore, while cars should be provided for expatriate employees in Bangkok, Hong Kong and Singapore. For the economic migrant, these major costs of living should be taken into account when moving overseas to better job opportunities, as they could have significant bearing on living standards and lifestyle.

Notes

1. Salt and Findlay (1989) argue that temporary movements of highly-skilled labour will increase with economic development and globalization as

greater specialization and harmonization of skills are required. Meanwhile, Ong *et al.* (1992) and Lewis (1993) argue that the internationalization of higher education has resulted in an international market for labour.

2. A detailed discussion on economic integration and the expansion of MNCs is provided by Shapiro (1996).

3. In Hungary, for instance, foreign investors are allowed to bring their own management teams to the country without any restrictions, due to a shortage of qualified managers.

4. See, for example, Lewis (1997).

5. According to Stuart (1991), each country has its own set of income, payroll, social security and other taxes, and income earned by expatriates is usually taxed according to the local tax rates. In some situations, employees may be taxed twice on all income, including allowances provided to maintain living standards, housing, transportation, moving expenses and dependent education, where no tax treaty exists between countries. In such instances, expatriate employees may require salary packages which include these items in lieu of allowances.

6. As an example, Fawcett *et al.* (1995) find that low wages in Mexico do not translate to a significant advantage for US MNCs, because its very low level of labour productivity (one-sixth that of the US) almost entirely offsets its low-cost labour advantage.

7. See, for instance, Abuaf and Jorion (1990), Diebold *et al.* (1991), Frenkel (1981), Lothian (1990), Manzur (1990), Officer (1976), Oh (1996) and Ong (1997).

8. One obvious example would be if the employee arranges to have his/her periodic mortgage instalments automatically paid from overseas.

9. Wages are calculated as actual hourly earnings in 12 selected manufacturing and service occupations, adjusted for the number of hours actually worked and weighted according to occupational distribution. These occupations comprise managerial and subordinate positions in service and manufacturing industries. Rather than just using selected managerial wages for a few industries, the aggregation of industry data in this instance addresses Oulton's (1994) concern that although there is a tendency for wages in any given country to grow at a similar rate across industries, the wage levels between industries differ significantly.

10. See Ong (1997) for a detailed discussion on the index-number problem in PPP research and the usefulness of the Big Mac Index.

11. Strictly speaking, of course, this holds if the employee consumes Big Macs only; however, empirical evidence has shown that Big Macs perform just as well as, if not better than, most other measures of PPP (Click, 1996; Cumby, 1996; Ong, 1997; and Pakko and Pollard, 1996).

12. This is consistent with Bennett's (1996) finding that expatriates from Europe working in the US generally earn much more than in their home countries, which results in a disincentive to return home.

13. Interestingly, real wages in Denmark in 1988 were much higher than justified by productivity. On the other hand, real wages in Hungary in

1994 were much lower relative to productivity. This supports Erickson and Kuruvilla's (1994) finding that the increasing differences in labour costs (in percentage terms) between the more and less-developed European countries in recent years is not matched by productivity growth. This suggests the existence of production efficiencies in the less-developed European countries.
14. Engel and Rogers (1996) had previously shown that distance plays an important role in explaining the price differences between locations.

References

Abuaf, N. and P. Jorion (1990) 'Purchasing Power Parity in the Long Run', *Journal of Finance*, vol. 45, pp. 157–74.

Balassa, B. (1964) 'The Purchasing-Power Parity Doctrine: A Reappraisal', *Journal of Political Economy*, vol. 72, pp. 584–96.

Bennett, L. (1996) 'The CBR Advisory Board Comments on: CEO Pay, Global Chaos, and a Possible Retreat from Benefits', *Compensation and Benefits Review*, vol. 28, pp. 58–65.

Chelminski, P. and J. K. S. Chong (1993) 'Labour Relations in Hungary: Managerial Implications for Western Investors', *Management Research News*, vol. 16, pp. 19–24.

Clements, K. W. and M. Semudram (1983) 'An International Comparison of the Price of Nontraded Goods', *Weltwirtschaftliches Archiv*, vol. 119, pp. 356–63.

Click, R. W. (1996) 'Contrarian MacParity', *Economics Letters*, vol. 53, pp. 209–12.

Cumby, R. E. (1996) 'Forecasting Exchange Rates and Relative Prices with the Hamburger Standard: Is What You Want What You Get with McParity?', NBER Working Paper Series, no. 5675, National Bureau of Economic Research, Cambridge, Massachusetts.

Delia-Loyle, D. (1992) 'Mission: Fill That Overseas Vacancy', *Global Trade*, vol. 112, p. 38.

Diebold, F. X., S. Husted and M. Rush (1991) 'Real Exchange Rates under the Gold Standard', *Journal of Political Economy*, vol. 99, pp. 1252–71.

Engel, C. and J. H. Rogers (1996) 'How Wide is the Border?', *American Economic Review*, vol. 86, pp. 1112–25.

Erickson, C. L. and S. Kuruvilla (1994) 'Labour Costs and the Social Dumping Debate in the European Union', *Industrial and Labour Relations Review*, vol. 48, pp. 28–47.

Fawcett, S. E., J. C. Taylor and S. R. Smith (1995) 'The Realities of Operating in Mexico: An Exploration of Manufacturing and Logistics Issues', *International Journal of Physical Distribution and Logistics Management*, vol. 25, pp. 48–68.

Frenkel, J. A. (1981) 'The Collapse of Purchasing Power Parities during the 1970s', *European Economic Review*, vol. 16, pp. 145–65.

Lewis, P. E. T. (1993) 'On the Move: The Changing Structure of the Singapore Labour Market', Asia Research Centre, Murdoch University, Western Australia.

Lewis, P. E. T. (1997) 'Temporary Movements of Professional Labour in East and South East Asia', *Asia Pacific Journal of Economics and Business*, vol. 1, pp. 24–40.

Lothian, J. R. (1990) 'A Century Plus of Japanese Exchange Rate Behaviour', *Japan and the World Economy*, vol. 2, pp. 47–70.

Lucas, R. E. (1988) 'On the Mechanics of Economic Development', *Journal of Monetary Economics*, vol. 22, pp. 3–42.

Manzur, M. (1990) 'An International Comparison of Prices and Exchange Rates: A New Test of Purchasing Power Parity', *Journal of International Money and Finance*, vol. 9, pp. 75–91.

Officer, L. H. (1976) 'The Purchasing-Power-Parity Theory of Exchange Rates: A Review Article', *IMF Staff Papers*, no. 23, pp. 1–60.

Oh, K. Y. (1996) 'Purchasing Power Parity and Unit Root Tests Using Panel Data', *Journal of International Money and Finance*, vol. 15, pp. 405–18.

Ong, L. L. (1997) 'Burgernomics: The Economics of the Big Mac Standard', *Journal of International Money and Finance*, vol. 16, pp. 865–78.

Ong, P. M., L. Cheng and L. Evans (1992) 'Migration of Highly Educated Asians and Global Dynamics', *Asian and Pacific Migration Journal*, vol. 1, pp. 543–67.

Oulton, N. (1994) 'Labour Productivity and Unit Labour Costs in Manufacturing: The UK and Its Competitors', *National Institute Economic Review*, no. 148, pp. 48–60.

Pakko, M. R. and P. S. Pollard (1996) 'For Here to Go? Purchasing Power Parity and the Big Mac', *Federal Reserve Bank of St. Louis Review*, vol. 78, pp. 3–21.

Salt, J. and A. Findlay (1989) 'International Migration of Highly Skilled Manpower: Theoretical and Development Issues', in *The Impact of International Migration on Developing Countries*, ed. R. J. Appleyard, pp. 159–80. Paris: OECD.

Shapiro, A. C. (1996) *Multinational Financial Management*, 5th edn. New Jersey: Prentice-Hall.

Stuart, P. (1991) 'Global Payroll – A Taxing Problem', *Personnel Journal*, vol. 10, pp. 80–90.

Prices and Earnings around the Globe, Union Bank of Switzerland, various issues.

The Economist, various issues.

6

Professors and Hamburgers:
An International Comparison of
Real Academic Salaries*

Co-authored with Jason D. Mitchell

In recent years, academic staff unions and associations have argued for higher salaries for academics on the grounds that existing salaries have not kept pace with inflation, are well-below commercial salaries and, most glaringly, are much lower than the salaries of their overseas counterparts. However, most international comparisons are made based on exchange rate conversions, which is inappropriate since purchasing power differentials are only reflected in exchange rates in the long term. Furthermore, the volatility of exchange rates makes such conversions highly inaccurate. In this chapter, we provide a comparison of real academic salaries by converting the nominal salaries in each country to their purchasing power equivalents, using the Big Mac Index. Our results show that real academic salaries are highest in Hong Kong and Singapore, relative to the developed countries, while Hong Kong tax and social security deductions are lowest. Furthermore, real salary levels, combined with intrinsic considerations such as the quality of life, indicate that Canada and New Zealand are unattractive places for visiting/migrating academics, while Australia and the US are relatively attractive. We suggest that our findings could be of use to policy-makers and academic unions in salary negotiations, as well as academics making relocation decisions.

---

*   Published in *Applied Economics*, vol. 32, pp. 869–76 (2000).

Introduction

Consider the following scenario: an American academic is invited to take up a similar position in Australia. His current position of, say, Associate Professor would be equivalent to that of a Senior Lecturer in Australia. His salary changes from US$49 695 to A$59 600. At the existing exchange rate of A$1.29 per US dollar, he quickly works out that his new salary would be equivalent to US$46 202. Not an offer worth considering, he concludes. Or is it?

The problem with the academic's calculation, of course, is that it presumes he earns his income in Australia and then spends it immediately in the US. That being the case, he would then definitely be worse off than his American colleagues who are earning more. However, since the relocating academic has to pay for his costs of living in the new country, it is the *purchasing power* of his new income that is the most important consideration. In other words, the comparison should be made between the *real* salaries in each country.

In the past, it has been argued that salaries tend to be higher in richer countries as a result of higher productivity and the relative immobility of labour (Balassa, 1964; Clements and Semudram, 1983). In today's increasingly integrated world economy, however, the expansion of trade in goods and services and the proliferation of multinational companies have resulted in an international market for skilled workers and professionals.[1] Cross-border education programmes as a result of increasing awareness of the importance of top-class education, along with fierce competition for research funds, point to the existence of an international market for academic talent. Thus, it follows that the salaries of these most skilful of professionals – academics – *should* tend to be equalized internationally, in real terms.

In recent years, academic staff unions and associations such as the Association of University Teachers (AUT) of Britain, the National Tertiary Education Industry Union (NTEU) of Australia and the American Association of University Professors (AAUP) have argued for higher salaries for academics on the grounds that existing salaries have not kept pace with inflation and are well-below commercial salaries.[2] More importantly, it has been highlighted that academics in some countries are disadvantaged compared to their overseas counterparts, in terms of salaries and other benefits. Often, however, salary comparisons are made based on exchange rate conversions.[3]

We argue that it is inappropriate to compare salaries using current exchange rates. This is because purchasing power differentials between countries are only reflected in exchange rates in the long run.[4] Moreover, the volatility of exchange rates makes such conversions highly inaccurate. Thus, the nominal salaries in each country should be converted to *purchasing power equivalents* in a standard currency, using a relative price index.

In this chapter, we provide a comparison of *real* academic salaries within a select group of countries where English-speaking academics would tend to migrate to or visit, since English is the main medium of instruction at the tertiary institutions in these countries. We propose using *The Economist's* Big Mac Index as the relative price index for several reasons: (1) the Big Mac hamburger is the 'perfect universal commodity' in that it is made to the same recipe in over 80 countries around the world and thus represents a standard basket of goods and services across countries;[5] (2) the concept is intuitively appealing and data are easily obtainable; and (3) the Index has been shown to perform just as well as most other measures of purchasing power parity (PPP).[6] Our comparisons are standardized using the US as a benchmark.[7] In addition, we also consider the quality of life in each of our sample countries to supplement the analysis.

The gross salaries data for 1997 are obtained for each position – for example Lecturer, Assistant Professor, and so on – from academic associations and unions, and individual universities in our sample countries, namely Australia, Britain, Canada, Hong Kong, New Zealand, Singapore, South Africa and the US. Meanwhile, corresponding Big Mac prices and exchange rates are obtained from *The Economist* magazine. Table 6.1 shows the academic salary scales for each country. Since Canada, Hong Kong and the US use different academic staff titles (column 1) to the system in Australia, Britain, New Zealand, Singapore and South Africa (column 2), we have equated them for comparison purposes and labelled the positions 'A' to 'E' to facilitate discussion.[8]

Our findings show that South Africa and Britain have the lowest real salaries; Hong Kong and Singapore have the highest. When taxes are considered, Hong Kong is even further ahead on an after-tax real salary basis, while Britain and Canada are worse off. Taking into account the quality of life as well as real salaries, Canada and New Zealand are unattractive destinations for academics, whereas

Table 6.1 Academic salaries: country averages, 1997 (in local currencies)

Position	Equivalent position	Country							
		US US$	Australia A$	Britain £	Canada C$	Hong Kong HK$	New Zealand NZ$	Singapore S$	South Africa Rand
A. Lecturer	Assistant Lecturer	34 755	37 285	18 088	38 481	434 040	36 931	N/A	50 659
B. Assistant Professor	Lecturer	41 041	49 432	26 482	48 208	659 810	48 321	66 578	76 123
C. Associate Professor	Senior Lecturer	49 695	59 600	32 487	61 415	910 855	64 295	104 695	96 306
D. Professor	Associate Professor	67 415	70 051	32 487	61 180	963 485	77 725	149 585	109 217
E. Chair Professor	Professor	N/A	85 868	33 882	N/A	1118 790	83 744	153 390	108 995

Notes

1 The data for the US are obtained from *Academe*, March–April 1997; the data for Australia are obtained from the 1997 Academic, Academic Research and Related Staff Agreement; the data for Britain are obtained from the Association of University Teachers (AUT); the data for Canada are obtained from *CAUT Bulletin ACPPU*, 3 March 1998; the data for Hong Kong and Singapore are obtained from the individual universities; the data for New Zealand are obtained from the Association of University Staff (AUS); the data for South Africa are obtained from the Association of Commonwealth Universities (ACU). The figures do not include additional allowances, compensation or loadings offered by some universities.

2 The figures for each position (excluding position E) are calculated as an average of the minimum and maximum salaries for that position in each country. The averages for Canada are calculated from the universities for which maximum and minimum salaries are available; the averages for South Africa are calculated from four of the major universities: Cape Town, Natal, Rand Afrikaans and Witwatersrand. For Canada, the position D figure of C$61 180 represents the average minimum.

3 Position E salary figures represent the average minimum salary for that position. In Australia, it is only a one-point scale.

4 N/A means the position is not available.

Australia and the US are attractive places to work. We suggest that these findings could be used by policy-makers and academic unions in salary negotiations. They could also be used by relocating academics to determine the attractiveness of positions abroad.

In the next section, we test for the PPP of academic salaries; specifically, comparisons are made based on US purchasing power equivalents. We then consider the quality of life in our sample countries, in conjunction with the standard of living made possible by the salaries offered. Concluding remarks are then presented.

Comparisons of purchasing power

Consider the situation where the US academic moves to another institution in Australia. A very important concern would be whether his purchasing power, and thus standard of living, can be maintained while overseas. For instance, if a Big Mac costs US$2.42 in the US and A$2.50 in Australia, then the academic would require a salary of $2.50 in Australia for every US$2.42 earned in the US in order to purchase a similar lifestyle in terms of Big Macs. If this is not the case, then the academic is said to have less or greater purchasing power in the foreign country. Strictly speaking, of course, this holds if the academic is to survive on Big Macs only. However, Big Macs are used as a rough and ready measure of purchasing power here, as discussed previously.

Table 6.2 shows the number of units of foreign currency the academic needs to earn for every US$1 earned in the US, in order to be

Table 6.2 The Big Mac Index, 1997

Country	Big Mac price (in local currency)	Big Mac PPP (in US$)	Actual exchange rate (in US$)
US	US$2.42	–	–
1. Australia	A$2.50	1.03	1.29
2. Britain	£1.81	0.75	0.61
3. Canada	C$2.88	1.19	1.39
4. Hong Kong	HK$9.90	4.09	7.75
5. New Zealand	NZ$3.25	1.34	1.45
6. Singapore	S$3.00	1.24	1.44
7. South Africa	R7.80	3.22	4.43

Source: *The Economist*, 12 April 1997, p. 75.

able to purchase equivalent numbers of Big Macs (maintain a similar lifestyle) in the respective foreign countries. The Big Mac PPP for each country is calculated as $s \equiv P_{BM}/P_{BM}^{\star}$, where P_{BM} and $P_{BM}^{\star}$ are the Big Mac prices in the foreign country and the US, respectively. We also show the obvious short-term differences between PPP and exchange rates in the table. As an example, an academic would have to earn A\$1.03 in Australia for every dollar earned in the US in order to be able maintain the same purchasing power in either country. If the actual exchange rate is used, the academic may think that he needs to earn A\$1.29 for every US dollar earned. In PPP terms, we say that the Australian dollar is *undervalued* relative to the US dollar. Thus, applying the Australian–US exchange rate would *overestimate* the cost of living in Australia. This highlights the fallacy of comparing salaries based on exchange rate conversions.

To further enhance salary comparisons across our sample countries, we deflate the nominal salary in the foreign country, P, by the Big Mac Index, s, to arrive at the purchasing power equivalent in US dollars:

$$p \equiv \frac{P}{s} \equiv \frac{P}{(P_{BM}/P_{BM}^{\star})}$$

The first panel in Table 6.3 gives the academic salaries in US PPP dollars. We see that the salary for position C in Australia would have purchased a lifestyle equivalent to US\$57 864 in the US. This is in contrast with a salary of US\$49 695 for a similar position in the US. Thus, the academic would actually be better off moving to the new job, despite the apparent disadvantage initially calculated using the exchange rate. Overall, we see that real salary levels are lowest in South Africa, while salaries in Hong Kong have the highest purchasing power by far.[9] Of the developed countries, Britain has the lowest real salaries, while Australian salaries are highest.

We subsequently calculate the relative real salaries as follows:

$$r \equiv \frac{p - P^{\star}}{P^{\star}} \equiv \frac{[P/(P_{BM}/P_{BM}^{\star})] - P^{\star}}{P^{\star}}$$

where $P^{\star}$ is the US academic salary. Thus, r is equal to zero if $P/P^{\star} = P_{BM}/P_{BM}^{\star}$; that is, the salaries are proportional to the costs of

Table 6.3 Real academic salaries: country averages, 1997

Position	Equivalent position	Country							
		USA	Australia	Britain	Canada	Hong Kong	New Zealand	Singapore	South Africa
		I. In US PPP dollars							
A. Lecturer	Assistant Lecturer	34 755	36 199	24 117	32 337	106 122	27 561	N/A	15 733
B. Assistant Professor	Lecturer	41 041	47 992	35 309	40 511	161 323	36 060	53 692	23 641
C. Associate Professor	Senior Lecturer	49 695	57 864	43 315	51 609	222 703	47 981	84 431	29 909
D. Professor	Associate Professor	67 415	68 010	43 315	51 412	235 571	58 004	120 633	33 918
E. Chair Professor	Professor	N/A	83 367	45 176	N/A	273 543	62 496	123 702	33 849
		II. As a percentage of the US							
A. Lecturer	Assistant Lecturer	100	104	69	93	305	79	N/A	45
B. Assistant Professor	Lecturer	100	117	86	99	393	88	131	58
C. Associate Professor	Senior Lecturer	100	116	87	104	448	97	170	60
D. Professor	Associate Professor	100	101	64	76	349	86	179	50
E. Chair Professor	Professor	N/A	124	67	N/A	406	93	183	50
Average		100	112	75	93	380	88	166	53

Notes
1 N/A means the position is not available.
2 Position E differentials for Australia, Britain, Hong Kong, New Zealand, Singapore and South Africa are calculated relative to position. D professorial salaries in the US.

living (as assumed by the Big Mac prices) in the two countries. Foreign salaries are said to have greater purchasing power than the US if r is greater than zero, and less purchasing power if r is less than zero. The percentage foreign salary differential from the US salary is $r \times 100$.

The second panel in Table 6.3 shows the relative real salaries between the US and the foreign countries, in percentage terms. The figures highlight the differences in real salaries across countries. The salaries in South Africa have between 40 and 55 per cent lower purchasing power than salaries in the US. British academics are also very undervalued, with real salaries up to 36 per cent lower than the US. Australian salaries are slightly higher than the US, while Canadian salaries are only marginally lower in most cases.[10] However, Professors in Canada earn 24 per cent less than their US counterparts. At the other end of the scale, Hong Kong and Singapore appear to value academic talent more than the developed countries. Hong Kong real salaries are between 200 and 300 per cent higher than the US for every position, while real salaries in Singapore are up to 83 per cent higher.

When the relative real salaries are averaged for each country, we see that Hong Kong is approximately 280 per cent higher than the US overall, South Africa is 47 per cent lower on average, while British salaries are 25 per cent below the US. Interestingly, with the exception of Australia and Singapore, the real salary differentials for each country relative to the US are the 'best' for position C. This suggests that the optimal time for an academic to visit/relocate to another country is while holding position C.

The caveat to our findings, of course, is that in addition to basic salaries, other compensation and benefits are sometimes available to expatriates. They include items such as (1) pensions, which consist of contributions made by the employer and employee which can be withdrawn upon retirement or permanent departure from the country in question; (2) medical aid schemes which have varying contributions and percentage of medical costs covered; (3) leave entitlements which encompass benefits such as annual, long-service, sabbatical and maternity leave; and (4) other benefits such as car and house loans, housing and housing allowances. To the extent that these compensation benefits differ across the various countries examined, there may be additional incentives other than salary to consider.[11]

Table 6.4   Index of gross and net salaries: country averages, 1988–94 (US index = 100)

Country	Gross salaries	Net salaries
US	100.0	100.0
Australia	72.1	71.2
Britain	75.4	72.6
Canada	94.0	88.8
Hong Kong	33.3	39.7
Singapore	30.8	30.5
South Africa	36.2	36.1

Source: *Prices and Earnings Around the Globe*, Union Bank of Switzerland, 1988/91/94.

Another major consideration is the different taxation system in each country. The academic needs to consider the taxation rates and social contributions which will be deducted in the destination country.[12] For instance, he may be better off going to a country which pays slightly lower salaries, but which has lower taxes, than he is moving to a country with high salaries but extremely unattractive tax rates. Table 6.4 shows the average gross and net salary levels over the 1988 to 1994 period for the countries in our sample.[13] We see that, on average, Australian, British and Canadian taxes and social security contributions take up a higher proportion of gross salaries than in the US, while deductions in Hong Kong are lower. Salary deductions in Singapore and South Africa are similar to the US.

Quality of life

In this section, we consider the quality of life in our sample countries. This is important because the academic may choose to trade off material well-being in the form of salary and other compensation and benefits for the quality of life offered by a particular country. For instance, the country which provides the highest standard of living may not be ideal by other intrinsic measures. *The Economist's* 'Places to Live' rankings, reproduced in Table 6.5, is based on four aspects of life – economic, social, cultural and political.

Of all the countries in our sample, we see that Australia is the best place to live overall: it has the best quality of life and real academic

Table 6.5   'Places to live' rankings

Country	Economic	Social	Cultural	Political	1993 Rank	1983 Rank
Switzerland	2	7	10	6	1	6
Germany	8	2	11	3	2	2
Spain	14	1	17	2	3	11
Sweden	10	2	6	8	4	7
Italy	4	4	3	14	5	5
Japan	1	6	13	17	6	4
Australia	11	9	2	5	7	3
United States	7	14	1	4	8	8
Britain	15	13	1	6	9	9
Hong Kong	3	10	15	11	10	N/A
France	11	3	11	15	11	1
New Zealand	21	12	4	1	12	N/A
Israel	11	5	6	20	13	12
Canada	19	8	8	10	14	10
Hungary	22	10	4	9	15	15
Mexico	6	19	8	13	16	13
Bahamas	9	18	13	16	17	14
South Korea	5	17	19	18	18	N/A
Russia	18	15	16	19	19	16
China	17	15	18	22	20	17
Brazil	20	21	20	12	21	20
India	16	20	21	21	22	22

Notes
1 For each aspect of life, eight criteria are set and the ranking is based on weightings obtained from a survey of editorial staff of *The Economist* located around the world.
2 The rankings for Singapore and South Africa are unavailable; 1983 rankings are unavailable for Hong Kong and New Zealand, denoted N/A.

Source: © The Economist Newspaper Limited, London, 25 December 1993, p. 39. Reproduced with permission.

salaries are the highest of the developed countries. Meanwhile, Canada and New Zealand are unattractive destinations for academics from Australia, Hong Kong and the US, with relatively lower quality of life and less purchasing power. The quality of life in Britain is quite attractive, despite its very low academic salaries.

Conclusion

An increasing awareness and demand for education in today's world has seen the growth of an international market for skilled educators.

It follows, then, that there should be a tendency for the price paid to these professionals to be equalized internationally. However, we argue that using exchange rates to convert salaries for comparison purposes is inappropriate since exchange rates only reflect relative purchasing power in the long run. Thus, a purchasing power parity approach using a relative price index is preferred.

In this chapter, we have compared the real academic salaries in countries where English is the main language of instruction at the tertiary level. We use the Big Mac Index as a measure of relative prices. Our results show that real academic salaries are highest in Hong Kong and Singapore, relative to the developed countries. This suggests that developing countries place a higher value on academic services. Real salaries appear to 'peak' at position C across most countries. When we take into account taxes and social security deductions from gross salaries, Hong Kong salaries are even more attractive. Overall, real salary levels, combined with intrinsic considerations such as the quality of life, indicate that Canada and New Zealand are unattractive places for visiting/migrating academics, while Australia and the US are relatively attractive.

Notes

1. See, for instance, Chelminski and Chong (1993) and Shapiro (1996).
2. See, for instance, 'Not So Good', *Academe*, March–April 1997; 'Scandalous Pay Levels in Higher Education', News Release, Association of University Teachers, 22 January 1998 (http://www.aut.org.uk/press98/pr98004.html, 1998).
3. The Association of Commonwealth Universities (ACU), for instance, currently compares academic salaries by converting all salaries using the US dollar exchange rate ('Survey of Academic Salaries and Conditions of Service', http://www.acu.ac.uk/chems/surveys/salary1.html, 1998).
4. See Abuaf and Jorion (1990), Diebold *et al.* (1991), Frenkel (1981), Lothian (1990), Manzur (1990), Officer (1976), Oh (1996) and Ong (1997).
5. The index-number problem in PPP research refers to the problem of making accurate comparisons of purchasing power differentials between countries using 'baskets' with different compositions of goods and services (Betton *et al.*, 1995; Froot and Rogoff, 1995; Officer, 1982).
6. See Click (1996), Cumby (1996), Ong (1997) and Pakko and Pollard (1996).
7. Another method of accounting for PPP, which has received wide attention recently, is the United Nations International Comparisons Project (ICP). According to Kravis (1986), the ICP system of income and purchasing power comparisons improves the measurement of countries' average incomes and the differences between them.

8. Positions equated per the Association of Commonwealth Universities (ACU) method ('Survey of Academic Salaries and Conditions of Service', http://www.acu.ac.uk/chems/surveys/saloview.html, 1998).
9. Although the cost of accommodation in Hong Kong may be exorbitant, housing is usually provided for expatriate academics by the respective tertiary institutions.
10. These results are different from the ACU survey ('Survey of Academic Salaries and Conditions of Service', http://www.acu.ac.uk/chems/surveys/saloview.html, 1998) which shows 'considerable similarity between the UK, Australia and New Zealand for most grades ...'
11. The ACU provides a comparison of staff benefits across its member countries on the website ('Survey of Academic Salaries and Conditions of Service', http://www.acu.ac.uk/chems/surveys/salary1.html, 1998).
12. Ong (1998) shows that the high tax rates and social security contributions in Europe mean that the purchasing power of net wages tends to be lower in European countries, while taxes are more favourable in Asian countries.
13. The gross salary figures are calculated on effective hourly wages in 12 different occupations, adjusted for differences in the number of hours worked and weighted according to occupational distribution; net after deducting taxes and social security contributions. Data for New Zealand are unavailable.

References

Abuaf, N. and P. Jorion (1990) 'Purchasing Power Parity in the Long Run', *Journal of Finance*, vol. 45, pp. 157–74.

Academe (1997) 'Not So Good', March–April 1997, pp. 12–88.

ACT (1998) 'Survey of Academic Salaries and Conditions of Service', Association of Commonwealth Universities, http://www.acu.ac.uk/chems/surveys/salary1.html and http://www.acu.ac.uk/chems/surveys/saloview.html (1998).

AUT (1998) 'Scandalous Pay Levels in Higher Education', News Release, Association of University Teachers, 22 January 1998, http://www.aut.org.uk/press98/pr98004.html, 1998.

Balassa, B. (1964) 'The Purchasing-Power Parity Doctrine: A Reappraisal', *Journal of Political Economy*, vol. 72, pp. 584–96.

Betton, S., M. D. Levi and R. Uppal (1995) 'Index-Induced Errors and Purchasing Power Parity: Bounding the Possible Bias', *Journal of International Financial Markets, Institutions and Money*, vol. 5, pp. 165–79.

CAUT (1998) 'A Tense Year for Contract Negotiations', *CAUT Bulletin ACPPU*, 3 March 1998.

Chelminski, P. and J. K. S. Chong (1993) 'Labour Relations in Hungary: Managerial Implications for Western Investors', *Management Research News*, vol. 16, pp. 19–24.

Click, R. W. (1996) 'Contrarian MacParity', *Economics Letters*, vol. 53, pp. 209–12.

Clements, K. W. and M. Semudram (1983) 'An International Comparison of the Price of Nontraded Goods', *Weltwirtschaftliches Archiv*, vol. 119, pp. 356–63.

Cumby, R. E. (1996) 'Forecasting Exchange Rates and Relative Prices with the Hamburger Standard: Is What You Want What You Get with McParity?', NBER Working Paper Series, no. 5675, National Bureau of Economic Research, Cambridge, Massachusetts.

Diebold, F. X., S. Husted and M. Rush (1991) 'Real Exchange Rates under the Gold Standard', *Journal of Political Economy*, vol. 99, pp. 1252–71.

Frenkel, J. A. (1981) 'The Collapse of Purchasing Power Parities during the 1970s', *European Economic Review*, vol. 16, pp. 145–65.

Froot, K. A. and K. Rogoff (1995) 'Perspectives on PPP and Long-Run Real Exchange Rates', in *Handbook of International Economics*, eds G. Grossman and K. Rogoff, vol. 3, pp. 1647–88. Amsterdam: North-Holland Press.

Kravis, I. B. (1986) 'The Three Faces of the International Comparison Project', *Research Observer*, vol. 1, pp. 3–26.

Lothian, J. R. (1990) 'A Century Plus of Japanese Exchange Rate Behavior', *Japan and the World Economy*, vol. 2, pp. 47–70.

Manzur, M. (1990) 'An International Comparison of Prices and Exchange Rates: A New Test of Purchasing Power Parity', *Journal of International Money and Finance*, vol. 9, pp. 75–91.

Officer, L. H. (1976) 'The Purchasing-Power-Parity Theory of Exchange Rates: A Review Article', *IMF Staff Papers*, vol. 23, pp. 1–60.

Officer, L. H. (1982) 'Purchasing Power Parity and Exchange Rates: Theory, Evidence and Relevance', in *Contemporary Studies in Economic and Financial Analysis*, eds E. I. Altman and I. Walter, vol. 35. Connecticut: JAI Press.

Oh, K. Y. (1996) 'Purchasing Power Parity and Unit Root Tests Using Panel Data', *Journal of International Money and Finance*, vol. 15, pp. 405–18.

Ong, L. L. (1997) 'Burgernomics: The Economics of the Big Mac Standard', *Journal of International Money and Finance*, vol. 16, pp. 865–78.

Ong, L. L. (1998) 'Big Mac and Wages to Go, Please: Comparing the Purchasing Power of Earnings abound the World', *Australian Journal of Labor Economics*, vol. 2, pp. 53–68.

Pakko, M. R. and P. S. Pollard (1996) 'For Here to Go? Purchasing Power Parity and the Big Mac', *Federal Reserve Bank of St. Louis Review*, vol. 78, pp. 3–21.

Prices and Earnings around the Globe, Union Bank of Switzerland, various issues.

Shapiro, A. (1996) *Multinational Financial Management*, 5th edn. New Jersey: Prentice-Hall International.

The Economist, various issues.

Index